JOE CELKO'S
SQL PUZZLES
& ANSWERS

JOE CELKO'S
SQL PUZZLES
& ANSWERS

Joe Celko

Morgan Kaufmann Publishers, Inc.
San Francisco, California

Senior Editor	Diane D. Cerra
Production Manager	Yonie Overton
Production Editor	Cheri Palmer
Editorial Assistant	Antonia Richmond
Cover and text design and spot illustrations	Carrie English, canary studios
Composition	Sybil Ihrig, VersaTech Associates
Copyeditor	Judith Abrahms
Proofreader	Jennifer McClain
Indexer	Ty Koontz
Printer	Courier Corporation

Morgan Kaufmann Publishers, Inc.
Editorial and Sales Office
340 Pine Street, Sixth Floor
San Francisco, CA 94104-3205
USA
Telephone   415 / 392-2665
Facsimile   415 / 982-2665
E-mail   mkp@mkp.com
Web site   http://www.mkp.com

Library of Congress Cataloging-in-Publication Data

Celko, Joe.
    [SQL puzzles & answers]
    Joe Celko's SQL puzzles & answers / Joe Celko.
        p.   cm.
    Includes index.
    ISBN 1-55860-453-7 (paper)
    1.   SQL (Computer program language)   I.   Title.
QA76.73.S67C46   1997
005.75'6—dc21   97-3991
                                               CIP

To chanticleer Michael—
*I now have a convincing argument
against solipsism for you.*

CONTENTS

How This All Happened

I have been writing columns for the computer trade press for over a decade, but people remember me only for the ones I write on databases and SQL. I have become a mouthpiece for ANSI/ISO standards, database programming techniques, and a champion database user throughout the world over the years. Or at least I like to think so.

My reputation was built on a column I began doing in *Database Programming & Design* (Miller Freeman) in January 1990 under the title "Celko on SQL," which ran until June 1992. I had done a few articles for the magazine before getting the column, so those gave me a following when I started. But the trick with a column is to get reader feedback—it isn't enough that people know you, they need to get involved with you. In short, you need a gimmick.

Some columns create a fictional set of characters and present a "mini-soap opera" from issue to issue; others present trade gossip. I considered this, but I cannot write dialog or fiction. My gimmick was a simple one I had used years before in columns in other publications: I ended each column with a programming problem for the reader to solve. The answer appeared in the following issue, along with some comments about the submissions. The reader response was quite good and the reason was obvious: programmers like to solve problems and to see their names in print!

DBMS magazine (M&T Publishing, since bought out by Miller Freeman) hired me as a full-time employee, so I stopped working as a freelance writer for *Database Programming & Design.* I began my column in *DBMS* in May 1992, under the title "SQL Explorer." It was renamed "SQL for Smarties" in April 1996, and I continue to write it today. I kept the puzzle at the end of each column, but my new editor wanted the answer in the same issue as the problem.

While I was working at *DBMS,* the Berlin Wall fell, Germany was reunified, and the Deutsche Bank called in a note they had against M&T's parent company in Germany. So the American operation was sold to Miller Freeman Publications. I suddenly had my old editors and friends back! They immediately fired me, of course; this was the

1980s and we had to downsize or upsize or rightsize, after all. But I kept my column and kept creating SQL puzzles for it.

I also did an SQL puzzle column in *Boxes and Arrows,* a small-circulation newsletter for DBAs and systems analysts who worked with IDMS and other older mainframe database products. I wrote my column there from October 1989 until the magazine folded in December 1994.

Why Puzzles?

Most of us had grown up on procedural languages and we were having a really hard time writing in nonprocedural SQL. Nobody had ever taught us how to think any other way. In fact, even today I earn a lot of my consulting money cleaning up systems where the SQL tables are used like sequential flat files while procedural code, hidden in triggers and stored procedures, replaces programs. As Artemus Ward observed, "It ain't what you don't know that kills you; it's what you know that ain't so."

This collection of puzzles is not merely a reprint of the old material as it appeared in the magazines. The explanations of the solutions—or even the problems!—were not as detailed as they might have been, because of space limitations. In many cases, there are several possible solutions, a few of which might have been discussed in a "Letters to the Editor" column months later, or not at all. This book is a chance for me to expand both the problems and the possible solutions in detail.

This book is also a chance for me to show how to think in SQL. When I was a Fortran programmer decades ago, we used to say (with pride!) that we could write anything in Fortran. Thus, we had commercial character-oriented math packages that used Fortran arrays to imitate Cobol, we faked pointers with Fortran arrays to imitate LISP, and so on.

In this fine tradition of "stupid programming tricks," I have added a few problems that should not have been done in SQL and worked them out in painful detail, not to show that they were possible, but to show the thought processes involved in attacking a problem from an SQL perspective.

We are now in the Age of the Internet, so I have been adding answers to these problems over time. In fact, at the risk of tarnishing my public image a little, I must admit that many of the original solutions have been cooked by other people over the years. (The term *cooked* is a puzzler's term for finding a better solution than the one the proposer of the problem presented.)

I did not try to organize the puzzles in chronological order, nor in order of complexity. There was no particular pattern to the order in which these problems appeared and I am not sure how to rate their complexity in comparison with one another. Instead, they are grouped according to an informal category scheme. I have tried to credit the persons involved with each problem, but if I missed someone, I apologize.

The Topic Areas

Rather than just produce a list of one problem-and-solution set after another, I have tried to break the book into chapters. Each chapter contains problems that have some common principle in their solution. I arbitrarily picked these five classifications:

1. Defining Data

2. Formatting Data

3. Selecting Data

4. Computing Things

5. Grouping Data

The trouble with my taxonomy is that one puzzle may have several solutions from different classes. Even worse, one solution may be classified in several ways because it uses more than one trick or technique. I try to explain what common characteristics each class has at the start of each chapter, but even this helps only marginally. I simply have to ask the reader to bear with me.

Corrections and Future Editions

I will be glad to receive corrections, new tricks and techniques, and other suggestions for future editions of this book. Send your ideas to

Joe Celko
235 Carter Avenue
Atlanta, GA 30317
   email: 71062.1056@compuserve.com

or contact me through the publisher, Morgan Kaufmann. You could see your name in print!

Acknowledgments

I'd like to thank Diane Cerra of Morgan Kaufmann, David Kalman and Maurice Frank of *DBMS* magazine, David Stodder of *Database Programming & Design,* Phil Chapnik of Miller Freeman, Frank Sweet of *Boxes and Arrows,* Richard Romley of Smith Barney for cooking so many of my puzzles, and all the people on CompuServe who sent me email all these years.

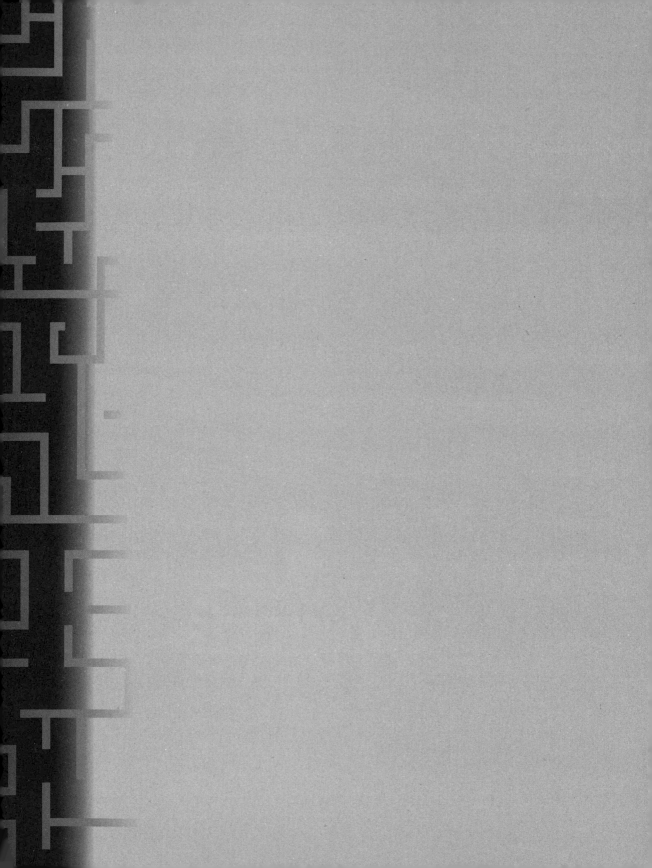

CHAPTER 1

Defining Data

WHEN SOMEONE GETS an SQL problem, the first thing they do is try to think of a query to answer it. Very often the problem lies in the data itself and a change to the tables will make the difficult problem into a simple one.

Denormalized Databases

There are several kinds of data problems. You will find that people denormalize databases in the name of performance, but pay for it in other ways. In particular, the database that was denormalized to make query A easier has just made queries B, C, and D difficult, unreliable, or impossible. There are solutions to denormalization problems:

1. Always be the guy who writes query A. This is not always practical.

2. Add CHECK() constraints to the tables to enforce the relationships that were destroyed by the denormalization. This is possible in SQL-92 because of two new features.

    The CHECK() constraints in one table can reference other tables in the same schema. The CHECK() constraint is still attached to one table and will be tested only when its table is modified.

SQL-92 also has a `CREATE ASSERTION` declaration, which creates a test that is attached to the schema as a whole and not to any particular table. While this feature is not widely implemented yet, it can do things that a `CHECK()` constraint cannot.

3. Use a `CREATE VIEW` statement to renormalize the table. Technically, the `VIEW` should not be needed in SQL-92 because of the extensive orthogonality of the language. In English, that means you could insert the `VIEW` definition in place of the `VIEW`'s name in any query.

   In practice, however, the `VIEW` is often a better idea. The `VIEW` will make reading the query easier and should not seriously affect performance. If the underlying base tables are changed, a modification to the `VIEW` will propagate to all the queries that use it. This will save you from the nightmare of looking for all the occurrences by hand yourself.

For the record, I am not opposed to denormalization, as are some other authors. I put it in the same category as major brain surgery; you don't do it as the first treatment attempt when the patient has a headache.

Bad Encoding Schemes

Bad encoding schemes are one of my pet peeves and I have a lot to say about them in my book *SQL for Smarties* (Morgan Kaufmann, 1995, ISBN 1-55860-323-9).

To appreciate what a difference a well-designed encoding scheme can make, compare the ease of use of the Hindu-Arabic numerals to the Roman numeral system. Before the Dewey decimal system, no two librarians arranged their stacks the same way, so you could not easily look up books among several libraries. In fact, if you didn't know how a particular librarian's mind worked, you couldn't find anything in the same library! Just for fun, try to think of a dozen places you could file a book on Irish church architecture in the Middle Ages. Today, if I want to look up all the books on a particular topic, I only need to know the Dewey decimal code and I can find it in any public library in North America.

Unfortunately, you do not often have the option of changing a bad encoding scheme in a database.

1 CREATING TABLES

Let's write some CREATE TABLE statements that are as complete as possible. This little exercise is important because SQL is a declarative language and you need to learn how to specify things in the database instead of in the code.

The table looks like this:

```
CREATE TABLE FiscalYearTable1
(fiscalyear SMALLINT,
 startdate DATE,
 enddate DATE);
```

It stores date ranges for determining what fiscal year any given date belongs to. For example, the federal government runs its fiscal year from October 1 until the end of September. The scalar subquery you would use to do this table lookup is

```
(SELECT F1.fiscalyear
   FROM FiscalYearTable1 AS F1
 WHERE outsidedate BETWEEN F1.startdate AND F1.enddate)
```

Your assignment is to add all the constraints you can think of to the table to guarantee that it contains only correct information.

While vendors all have different date and time functions, let's assume that all we have is the SQL-92 temporal arithmetic and the function EXTRACT ([YEAR | MONTH | DAY] FROM <date expression>), which returns an integer that represents a field within a date.

Answer

1. First things first; make all the columns NOT NULL, since there is no good reason to allow them to be NULL.

2. Most SQL programmers immediately think in terms of adding a PRIMARY KEY, so you might add the constraint PRIMARY KEY (fiscalyear, startdate, enddate), because the fiscal year

is really another name for the pair (`startdate`, `enddate`). This is not enough, because it would allow this sort of error:

```
(1995, '1994-10-01', '1995-09-30')
(1996, '1995-10-01', '1996-08-30') <== error!
(1997, '1996-10-01', '1997-09-30')
(1998, '1997-10-01', '1997-09-30')
```

You could continue along the same lines and fix some problems by adding the constraints UNIQUE (`fiscalyear`), UNIQUE (`startdate`), and UNIQUE (`enddate`), since we do not want duplicate dates in any of those columns.

3. The constraint that almost everyone forgets to add because it is so obvious:

```
CHECK (startdate <= enddate)
```

4. A better way would be to use the constraint PRIMARY KEY (`fiscalyear`), as before, but then, since the start and end dates are the same within each year, you could use constraints on those column declarations:

```
CREATE TABLE FiscalYearTable1
(fiscalyear SMALLINT NOT NULL PRIMARY KEY,
 startdate DATE NOT NULL,
 CONSTRAINT valid_startdate
    CHECK ((EXTRACT (YEAR FROM startdate) = fiscalyear - 1)
           AND (EXTRACT (MONTH FROM startdate) = 10)
           AND CHECK (EXTRACT (DAY FROM startdate) = 01)),
 enddate DATE NOT NULL,
 CONSTRAINT valid_enddate
   CHECK ((EXTRACT (YEAR FROM enddate) = fiscalyear)
    AND (EXTRACT (MONTH FROM enddate) = 09)
    AND (EXTRACT (DAY FROM enddate) = 30)));
```

You could argue for making each predicate a separate constraint to give more detailed error messages. The predicates on the year components of the startdate and enddate columns also guarantee uniqueness, because they are derived from fiscalyear, which is unique.

5. Unfortunately, the method just given does not work for all companies. Many companies have an elaborate set of rules that involve taking into account the weeks, weekends, and weekdays involved. They do this to arrive at exactly 360 days or 52 weeks in their accounting year. In fact, there is a fairly standard accounting practice of using a "4 weeks, 4 weeks, 5 weeks" quarter, with some fudging at the end of the year; you can have a leftover week of between 3 and 11 days. The answer is a FiscalMonth table along the same lines as this FiscalYear example.

A constraint that will work surprisingly well for such cases is

```
CHECK ((enddate - startdate) = INTERVAL 359 DAYS)
```

Here, you adjust the number of days to fit your rules (e.g., 52 weeks * 7 days = 364 days). If the rules allow some variation in the size of the fiscal year, replace the equality test with a BETWEEN predicate.

Now, true confession time. When I have to load such a table in a database, I get out my copy of SuperCalc and build a table using the functions in my spreadsheet. Spreadsheets have much better temporal functions than databases.

PUZZLE

2 ABSENTEE

This problem was presented on the MS-ACCESS Forum on CompuServe by Jim Chupella. He wanted to create a database that tracks employee absentee rates. Here is the table you will use:

```
CREATE TABLE Absenteeism
(empid INTEGER NOT NULL REFERENCES Employees (empid),
 deptid INTEGER NOT NULL REFERENCES Departments (deptid),
 missdate DATE NOT NULL,
 reason CHAR (40) NOT NULL REFERENCES ExcuseList (reason),
 severity INTEGER NOT NULL CHECK (severity BETWEEN 1 AND 4),
 PRIMARY KEY (empid, deptid, missdate));
```

An employee ID number and department code identify each employee. The reason field is a short text explanation for the absence (for example, "hit by beer truck," "bad hair day," and so on) that you pull from an ever-growing and imaginative list, and severity is a point system that scores the penalty associated with the absence.

If an employee accrues 40 severity points within a one-year period, you automatically discharge that employee. If an employee is absent more than one day in a row, it is charged as a long-term illness, not as a typical absence. The employee does not receive a severity point on the second, third, or later days, nor do those days count toward his/her total absenteeism.

Your job is to write SQL to enforce these two business rules, changing the schema if necessary.

 ### Answer #1

Looking at the first rule on discharging employees, the most common design error is to try to drop the second, third, and later days from the table. This approach messes up queries that count sick days, and makes chains of sick days very difficult to find.

The trick is to allow a score of zero severity, so you can track the long-term illness of an employee in the Absenteeism table. Simply

change the severity declaration to "CHECK (severity BETWEEN
0 AND 4)" so that you can give a zero to those absences that do
not count.

```
UPDATE Absenteeism
   SET severity = 0,
       reason = 'long term illness'
 WHERE EXISTS
         (SELECT *
            FROM Absenteeism AS A2
           WHERE Absenteeism.empid = A2.empid
             AND Absenteeism.missdate = (A2.missdate - INTERVAL
             1 DAY));
```

When a new row is inserted, this update will look for another absence on the day before and change its severity score and reason in
accordance with your first rule.

The second rule for firing an employee requires that you know what
his/her current point score is. You would write that query as follows:

```
SELECT empid, SUM(severity)
  FROM Absenteeism
 GROUP BY empid;
```

This is the basis for a grouped subquery in the DELETE FROM
statement you finally want. The employees with less than 40 points
will return a NULL, and the test will fail.

```
DELETE FROM Employees
 WHERE empid = (SELECT A1.empid
                  FROM Absenteeism AS A1
                 WHERE A1.empid = Employees.empid
                 GROUP BY A1.empid
                HAVING SUM(severity) >= 40);
```

The GROUP BY clause is not really needed in SQL-92, but some
older SQL implementations require it.

Answer #2

Bert Scalzo, a senior instructor for Oracle Corporation in Powell, Ohio, pointed out that the puzzle solution had two flaws and room for performance improvements.

The flaws are quite simple. First, the subquery does not check for employees accruing 40 or more severity points within a one-year period, as required. It requires the addition of a date range check in the WHERE clause:

```
DELETE FROM Employees
 WHERE empid = (SELECT A1.empid
                  FROM Absenteeism AS A1
                 WHERE A1.empid = Employees.empid
                   AND missdate
                       BETWEEN CURRENT_TIMESTAMP
                       AND CURRENT_TIMESTAMP
                           - INTERVAL 365 DAYS
                 GROUP BY A1.empid
                HAVING SUM(severity) >= 40);
```

Second, this SQL code deletes only offending employees and not their absenteeisms. The related absenteeisms must be either explicitly or implicitly deleted as well. You could replicate the above deletion for the Absenteeism table. However, the best solution is to add a cascading deletion clause to the Absenteeism table declaration:

```
CREATE TABLE Absenteeism
    (   ...
        empid               INTEGER NOT NULL
                            REFERENCES Employees(empid)
                            ON DELETE CASCADE,
    ...);
```

The performance suggestions are based on some assumptions. If you can safely assume that the UPDATE is run regularly and people do not change their departments while they are absent, you can improve the UPDATE command's subquery:

```
UPDATE Absenteeism AS A1
   SET severity = 0,
       reason = 'long term illness'
 WHERE EXISTS
      (SELECT *
         FROM absenteeism as A2
        WHERE A1.empid = A2.empid
          AND A1.deptid = A2.deptid
          AND (A1.missdate + INTERVAL 1 DAY) = A2.missdate);
```

In Oracle, the asterisk can be replaced with a constant to eliminate the data dictionary lookups for the selected columns; the compiler will satisfy the query by accessing only the index and the actual data. Second, if you add the deptid and place the missed date calculation on the opposite side, the execution plan switches from an index range scan to an index unique scan.

The use of a constant in the SELECT clause instead of an asterisk is a good trick, but it depends on your SQL. Some optimizers will see that this is an EXISTS() predicate, which means that the system can replace the asterisk with one or more columns of its own choice. The optimizer then looks at which columns in the WHERE clause have indexes, and uses the best indexes for the job.

There is still a problem with long-term illnesses that span weeks. The current situation is that if you want to spend your weekends being sick, that is fine with the company. This is not a very nice place to work. If an employee reports off on Friday of week number 1, all of week number 2, and just Monday of week number 3, the UPDATE will catch only the five days from week number 2 as long-term illness. The Friday and Monday will show up as sick days with severity codes. The subquery in the UPDATE requires additional changes to the missed-date chaining.

I would avoid problems with weekends by having a code for scheduled days off (weekends, holidays, vacation, and so on) that carry a severity code of zero. A business that has people working weekend shifts would need such codes.

The boss could manually change the Saturday and Sunday "weekend" codes to "long-term illness" to get the UPDATE to work the way you described. This same trick would also prevent you from losing scheduled vacation time if you got the plague just before going on a cruise. If the boss is a real sweetheart, he or she could also add compensation days for the lost weekends with zero severity to the table, or reschedule an employee's vacation by adding absenteeisms dated in the future.

While I agreed that I had left out the aging on the dates missed, I will argue that it would be better to have another DELETE FROM statement that removes the year-old rows from the Absenteeism table, to keep the size of the table as small as possible.

The expression (BETWEEN CURRENT_TIMESTAMP AND CURRENT_TIMESTAMP - INTERVAL 365 DAYS) could also be (BETWEEN CURRENT_TIMESTAMP AND CURRENT_TIMESTAMP - INTERVAL 1 YEAR) so that the system would handle leap years. Better yet, DB2 and some other SQL products have an AGE(date1) function, which returns the age in years of something that happened on the date parameter. You would then write (AGE(missdate) >= 1) instead.

If you assume that the empid is declared UNIQUE, it will have a unique index on it in the Employee table. But I don't see what using the deptid will buy you in the Absenteeism table.

PUZZLE

3
ANESTHESIA

Leonard C. Medal came up with this nifty little problem a couple of years ago. Anesthesiologists administer anesthesia during surgery in a hospital's operating rooms. Information about each anesthesia procedure is recorded in a table.

Procs

proc_id	anest	start_time	end_time
10	'Baker'	08:00	11:00
20	'Baker'	09:00	13:00
30	'Dow'	09:00	15:30
40	'Dow'	08:00	13:30
50	'Dow'	10:00	11:30
60	'Dow'	12:30	13:30
70	'Dow'	13:30	14:30
80	'Dow'	18:00	19:00

Note that some of the times for a given anesthesiologist overlap. This is not a mistake. Anesthesiologists, unlike surgeons, can move from one operating room to another while surgeries are under way, checking on each patient in turn, adjusting dosages, and leaving junior doctors and anesthesia nurses to monitor the patients on a minute-to-minute basis.

Payment for the anesthesiologist is per procedure, but there's a catch. There's a sliding scale for remuneration for each procedure, based on the maximum instantaneous count of simultaneous procedures that an anesthesiologist has under way. The higher this count, the lower the amount paid for the procedure.

For example, for procedure #10, for each instant during that procedure, Dr. Baker counts up the total number of procedures he was concurrently involved in. This maximum count for procedure #10 is 2. Based on the concurrency rules, Dr. Baker is paid 75% of the fee for procedure #10.

The problem, then, is to determine for each procedure, over its duration, the *maximum, instantaneous count* of procedures carried out by the anesthesiologist.

We can derive the answer graphically at first to get a better understanding of the problem.

Example 1 shows two overlapping procedures. The upper, Gantt-like graph displays the elapsed time of the procedure we are evaluating (the subject procedure) and all the doctor's other procedures that overlap it in time.

The lower graph (Total procedures in progress) shows how many procedures are under way at each moment. It helps to think of a slide-rule hairline moving from left to right over the Gantt chart while each procedure's start or end is plotted stepwise on the lower chart.

We can see in example 1 by inspection that the maximum is 2.

Example 1—Dr. Baker, Proc #10

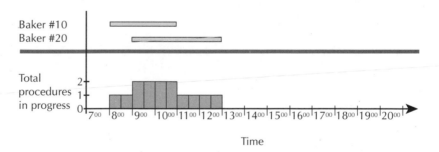

Time

Example 2 shows a more complex set of overlapping procedures, but the principle is the same. The maximum, which occurs twice, is 3.

Example 2—Dr. Dow, Proc #30

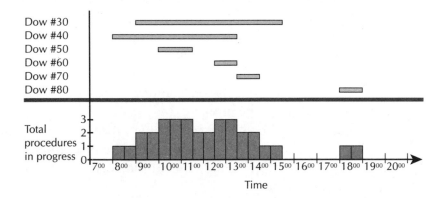

Time

Note that the correct answer is not the number of overlapping procedures but the maximum instantaneous count.

The puzzle is how to do this for each procedure using SQL. Here is the desired result for the sample data:

subject_proc	max_inst_count
10	2
20	2
30	3
40	3
50	3
60	3
70	2
80	1

Answer

The first step is to convert each procedure into two Events—a start Event and an end Event—and put them in a view. The UNION operator appends the set of end Events to the set of start Events. A (+1) indicates a start Event and a (−1) indicates an end Event.

The WHERE clauses ensure that the procedures compared overlap and are for the same anesthesiologist. The NOT condition eliminates procedures that do not overlap the subject procedure.

```
CREATE VIEW Events AS
   SELECT P1.proc_id AS subject_proc,
          P2.proc_id AS comparison_proc,
          P1.anest,
          P2.start_time AS event_time,
          +1 AS event_type
     FROM Procs AS P1, Procs AS P2
    WHERE P1.anest = P2.anest
      AND NOT (P2.end_time <= P1.start_time
               OR P2.start_time >= P1.end_time)
  UNION
   SELECT P1.proc_id AS subject_proc,
          P2.proc_id AS comparison_proc,
          P1.anest,
          P2.end_time AS event_time,
          -1 AS event_type
     FROM Procs AS P1, Procs AS P2
    WHERE P1.anest = P2.anest
      AND NOT (P2.end_time <= P1.start_time
               OR P2.start_time >= P1.end_time);
```

The result is this VIEW, shown here for procedure #10 only and sorted by event_time for clarity:

Events

subject_proc	comparison_proc	anest	event_time	event_type
10	10	Baker	08:00	+1
10	20	Baker	09:00	+1
10	10	Baker	11:00	−1
10	20	Baker	13:00	−1

Now, for each set of Events with the same subject_proc id, we can compute for each event the sum of the event_types for Events that occur earlier. This series of backward-looking sums gives us the values represented by each step in the step charts.

```
SELECT E1.subject_proc, E1.event_time,
    (SELECT SUM(E2.event_type)
       FROM Events AS E2
     WHERE E2.subject_proc = E1.subject_proc
       AND E2.event_time < E1.event_time)
           AS instantaneous_count
  FROM Events AS E1
 ORDER BY E1.subject_proc, E1.event_time;
```

The result of this query is shown here for procedure #10 only.

subject_proc	instantaneous_count
10	NULL
10	1
10	2
10	1

You could put this result set into a VIEW called Concurrencies, then query the VIEW to get the maximum instantaneous count for each subject procedure using this statement:

```
SELECT   subject_proc,
         MAX(instantaneous_count) AS max_inst
   FROM  Concurrencies
GROUP BY subject_proc
ORDER BY subject_proc;
```

But you could also extract the desired result directly from the Events VIEW. You could do this by merging the two SELECT statements:

```
SELECT E1.subject_proc,
   MAX((SELECT SUM(E2.event_type)
          FROM Events AS E2
        WHERE E2.subject_proc = E1.subject_proc
         AND E2.event_time < E1.event_time))
           AS max_inst_count
 FROM Events AS E1
 GROUP BY F1.subject_proc
 ORDER BY E1.subject_proc;
```

SECURITY BADGES

As a result of rightsizing at your company, you are now the security officer and database administrator. You want to produce a list of employees and their active security-badge numbers. Each employee can have many badges, depending on where that person is currently working, but only one of these badges will be active at a time. The default is that the most recently issued badge is assumed to be active. The badge numbers are random, to prevent counterfeiting. Your task is to produce a list of employees, each with the relevant active badge number. Let's use 'A' for active and 'I' for inactive badge status.

Answer

From the specification, you know that each employee can have all but one badge set to inactive, so it would be nice to enforce that at the database level.

```
CREATE TABLE Employees
(empno INTEGER PRIMARY KEY,
 empname CHAR(30) NOT NULL,
 ...);
CREATE TABLE Badges
(badgeno INTEGER NOT NULL
 empno INTEGER NOT NULL REFERENCES Employees (empno),
 issuedate DATE NOT NULL,
 status CHAR(1) NOT NULL CHECK (status IN ('A', 'I')),
    ...
 CHECK (1 = ALL (SELECT COUNT(status)
                FROM Badges
                WHERE status = 'A'
                GROUP BY empno))
 );
```

To be fair, I must point out that a lot of SQL implementations will gag on the final CHECK( ) clause on Badges because of the self-reference in the predicate, but it is legal SQL-92 syntax. You could drop that CHECK( ) clause and allow an employee to have no active badge. That, however, would mean that you need a way of updating the status of the most recently issued badge to 'A' for the employees.

```
UPDATE Badges
   SET status = 'A'
 WHERE ('I' = ALL (SELECT status
                     FROM Badges AS B1
                    WHERE empno = B1.empno))
   AND (issuedate = (SELECT MAX (issuedate)
                       FROM Badges AS B2
                      WHERE empno = B2.empno));
```

Again, I must point out that a lot of SQL implementations will also gag on this update because of the correlation names. The rule in SQL-92 is that the scope of the table name in the UPDATE is the whole statement, and the current row is used for the column values referenced. Therefore, you have to use the correlation names to see the rest of the table. Now the original query is really easy:

```
SELECT Employees.empno, empname, badgeno
   FROM Employees, Badges
 WHERE Badges.empno = Employees.empno
   AND Status = 'A';
```

PUZZLE

5 FORMATTING YOUR DATA

How do you ensure that a column will have a single alphabetic character string in it? (That means no spaces, no numbers, and no special characters.)

In most older procedural languages, you have to declare data fields with format constraints in the file declarations. The obvious examples are Cobol and PL/I. Another approach is to use a template to filter the data as you read; the Fortran-style FORMAT statement is the best-known example.

SQL has made a strong effort to separate the logical view of data from the physical representation of it, so you don't get much help with specifying the physical layout of your data. When a programmer at our little shop came to me with this one, I came up with some really bad first tries using substrings and BETWEEN predicates in a CHECK( ) clause that was longer than the whole schema declaration.

Answer

I keep telling people to think in terms of whole sets and not in a "record-at-a-time" mindset when they write SQL. The trick is to think in terms of whole strings and not a character at a time. Here is the answer:

```
CREATE TABLE Foobar
(alpha_only VARCHAR(6)
          CHECK ((UPPERCASE(TRIM(alpha_only)) || 'AAAAA')
               BETWEEN 'AAAAAA' AND 'ZZZZZZ'),
...
);
```

First we prune off any blanks around the string—and leave any that are inside it. TRIM( ) is the SQL-92 standard for removing extra characters from the right or left side of the string in its parameter. You will find that most SQL products have a version of TRIM( ), which will do the job.

Next we concatenate the string 'AAAAA' to it; notice that this is five letters long (one less than the length of the column), so if the original string was empty, this new string will fail the BETWEEN predicate. If you want to allow a blank string, make the string of 'A' characters the same length as the column. The third step is to uppercase the string and then to see if the results are in the alphabetic range.

This trick can be generalized. For example, if you wanted a column to contain three letters followed by three digits, you would remove the first three characters and apply this same CHECK() constraint.

PUZZLE

6   HOTEL RESERVATIONS

Scott Gammans posted a version of the following problem on the WATCOM Forum on CompuServe. Suppose you are the clerk at Hotel SQL and you have the following table:

```
CREATE TABLE Hotel
(roomno SMALLINT NOT NULL,
 arrival DATE NOT NULL,
 departure DATE NOT NULL,
 guest CHAR(30),
 PRIMARY KEY (roomno, arrival),
 CHECK (departure >= arrival));
```

Right now, the CHECK( ) clause enforces the data-integrity constraint that you cannot leave before you have arrived, but you want more. How do you enforce the rule that you cannot add a reservation that has an arrival date conflicting with the prior departure date for a given room?

Answer

One solution requires a product to have the capability of using fairly complex SQL in the CHECK( ) clause, so you'll find that a lot of implementations do not support it.

```
CREATE TABLE Hotel
(roomno SMALLINT NOT NULL,
 arrival DATE NOT NULL,
 departure DATE NOT NULL,
 guest CHAR(30),
 PRIMARY KEY (roomno, arrival),
 CHECK (departure >= arrival),
 CHECK (NOT EXISTS
        (SELECT *
```

```
      FROM Hotel AS H1, Hotel AS H2
     WHERE H1.roomno = H2.roomno
       AND H1.arrival
           BETWEEN H2.arrival AND H2.departure))
);
```

Another solution is to redesign the table, giving a row for each day and each room, thus:

```
CREATE TABLE Hotel
(roomno SMALLINT NOT NULL,
 occupydate DATE NOT NULL,
 guest CHAR(30) NOT NULL,
 PRIMARY KEY (roomno, occupydate));
```

This does not need any check clauses, but it can take up a lot of disk space. You will also need to find a way in the INSERT INTO statements to make sure that you put in all the room days without any gaps.

Incidentally, in full SQL-92 you will have an OVERLAPS predicate that tests to see whether two time intervals overlap a temporal version of the BETWEEN predicate currently in SQL implementations. However, no product has implemented it yet.

PUZZLE

7 PORTFOLIO

Steve Tilson sent this problem to me in November 1995:

"I have a puzzle for you. Perhaps I cannot see the forest for the trees here, but this seems like a real challenge to solve in an elegant manner that does not result in numerous circular references.

"Although this puzzle seems to be an entire system, my question is whether or not there is a way to eliminate the apparent circular references within the table design phase.

"Let's say you must keep track of Portfolios in an organization for lookup or recall. There are various attributes attached, but only certain items are pertinent to the puzzle:

```
CREATE TABLE Portfolios
(file_id INTEGER NOT NULL PRIMARY KEY,
 issue_date DATE NOT NULL,
 superseded_by INTEGER NOT NULL REFERENCES Portfolios.file_id,
 supersedes INTEGER NOT NULL REFERENCES Portfolios.file_id)
```

"Here is the puzzle:

- You need to keep track of which portfolio superseded this portfolio.

- You need to keep track of which portfolio this portfolio has superseded.

- You need to be able to reinstate a portfolio (which has the effect of superseding a portfolio or of creating a portfolio chain that has a circular reference).

- You can track the dates by virtue of the `issue_date`, but another thorny issue results if a portfolio is reinstated!

- You need to be able to SELECT the most current portfolio, regardless of the portfolio in a SELECT statement.

- You need to be able to reproduce an audit trail for a chain of documents."

Answer

Steve is still thinking in terms of pointer chains and procedural languages. Shame on him! We know this is a problem that deals with ordinal numbering, because we have the "giveaway" words *successor* and *predecessor* in the specification. Let's apply what we just discussed about nested sets instead.

First create a table to hold all the information on each file:

```
CREATE TABLE Portfolios
(file_id INTEGER NOT NULL PRIMARY KEY,
  other_stuff .... );
```

Then create a table to hold the succession of the documents, with two special columns, chain and next, in it:

```
CREATE TABLE Succession
(chain INTEGER NOT NULL,
 next INTEGER NOT NULL CHECK (next >= 0) DEFAULT 0,
 file_id INTEGER NOT NULL REFERENCES Portfolios(file_id),
 suc_date NOT NULL,
 PRIMARY KEY(chain, next));
```

Imagine that the original document is the zero point on a line. The next document, which supersedes it, is a circle drawn around the point. The third document in the chain of succession is a second circle drawn around the first circle, and so forth. We show these nested sets with the next value, flattening the circles onto the number line starting at zero.

You have to create the new document row in Portfolios, then the succession table entry. The value of next in the successor is 1 greater than the highest next value in the chain. Nested sets!!

Here is some sample data where a chain of '22?' and '32?' documents is superseded by a single document, 999:

```
CREATE TABLE Portfolios
(file_id INTEGER NOT NULL PRIMARY KEY,
 stuff CHAR(15) NOT NULL);
```

```
INSERT INTO Portfolios VALUES (222, 'stuff');
INSERT INTO Portfolios VALUES (223, 'old stuff');
INSERT INTO Portfolios VALUES (224, 'new stuff');
INSERT INTO Portfolios VALUES (225, 'borrowed stuff');
INSERT INTO Portfolios VALUES (322, 'blue stuff');
INSERT INTO Portfolios VALUES (323, 'purple stuff');
INSERT INTO Portfolios VALUES (324, 'red stuff');
INSERT INTO Portfolios VALUES (325, 'green stuff');
INSERT INTO Portfolios VALUES (999, 'yellow stuff');

CREATE TABLE Succession
(chain INTEGER NOT NULL,
 next INTEGER NOT NULL,
 file_id INTEGER NOT NULL REFERENCES Portfolios(file_id),
 suc_date NOT NULL,
 PRIMARY KEY(chain, next));

INSERT INTO Succession VALUES (1, 0, 222, '1995-11-01');
INSERT INTO Succession VALUES (1, 1, 223, '1995-11-02');
INSERT INTO Succession VALUES (1, 2, 224, '1995-11-04');
INSERT INTO Succession VALUES (1, 3, 225, '1995-11-05');

INSERT INTO Succession VALUES (2, 0, 322, '1995-11-01');
INSERT INTO Succession VALUES (2, 1, 323, '1995-11-02');
INSERT INTO Succession VALUES (2, 2, 324, '1995-11-04');
INSERT INTO Succession VALUES (2, 3, 322, '1995-11-05');
INSERT INTO Succession VALUES (2, 4, 323, '1995-11-12');
INSERT INTO Succession VALUES (1, 3, 999, '1995-11-25');
INSERT INTO Succession VALUES (2, 5, 999, '1995-11-25');
```

To answer your queries:

- You need to be able to SELECT the most current portfolio regardless of the portfolio in a SELECT statement.

```
SELECT DISTINCT P1.file_id, stuff, suc_date
  FROM Portfolios AS P1, Succession AS S1
 WHERE P1.file_id = S1.file_id
   AND next = (SELECT MAX(next)
                 FROM Succession AS S2
                WHERE S1.chain= S2.chain);
```

I have to use the SELECT DISTINCT option in case two or more chains were superseded by a single document.

- You need to be able to reproduce an audit trail for a chain of documents.

```
SELECT chain, next, P1.file_id, stuff, suc_date
  FROM Portfolios AS P1, Succession AS S1
 WHERE S1.file_id = P1.file_id
 ORDER BY chain, next;
```

- You need to keep track of which portfolio superseded this portfolio.

```
SELECT S1.file_id, ' superseded ',
       S2.file_id, ' on ', S2.suc_date
  FROM Succession AS S1, Succession AS S2
 WHERE S1.chain = S2.chain
   AND S1.next = S2.next + 1
   AND S1.file_id = :my_file_id;
   -- remove for all portfolios
```

- You need to be able to reinstate a portfolio, which has the effect of superseding a portfolio or of creating a portfolio chain that has a circular reference.

```
BEGIN
-- Create a row for the new document
INSERT INTO Portfolios VALUES (1000, 'sticky stuff');
```

```
-- adds new_file_id to chain with :old_file_id anywhere
-- in it.
INSERT INTO Succession (chain, next, file_id, suc_date)
VALUES ((SELECT DISTINCT chain
           FROM Succession AS S1
          WHERE S1.file_id = :old_file_id),
         (SELECT MAX(next) + 1
            FROM Succession AS S1
           WHERE S1.chain = (SELECT DISTINCT chain
                               FROM Succession AS S2
                              WHERE file_id =
                              :my_file_id)),
       :new_file_id, :new_suc_date);
END;
```

The problem here is that I allowed for a single file to supersede more than one existing file and for more than one file to supersede a single existing file. My chains are not really all that linear. This code blows up if :old_file_id is in more than one chain. You can fix it by asking for the chain number or the file_id of the document that the new file supersedes, but the SQL is ugly and I don't have time to work it out right now. You can try it.

- You can track the dates by looking at the issue_date, but another thorny issue results if a portfolio is reinstated!

  No big deal with this schema. Do a SELECT on any particular file_id and look at the dates and next column to get the chain of events. You did not say whether the succession date column values have to be in increasing order, along with the next column values. Is that true? If so, we need to add another CHECK() clause to handle this.

PUZZLE

8   SCHEDULING PRINTERS

Yogesh Chacha ran into a problem and sent it to me on CompuServe on September 12, 1996. Users in his shop usually end up using the wrong printer for printout; thus, they decided to include a new table in the system that will derive the correct printer for each user at run-time. Their table looked like this:

```
CREATE TABLE PrinterControl
(userid CHAR(20),
 printer_name CHAR(20) NOT NULL,
 description CHAR(40) NOT NULL);
```

The rules of operation are:

1. If the user has an entry in the table, he will pick the corresponding printer_name.

2. If the user is not in the table, he is supposed to use one of the printers whose userid is NULL.

Now consider the following example:

PrinterControl

userid	printer_name	description
'chacha'	'LPT1'	'First floor's printer'
'lee'	'LPT2'	'Second floor's printer'
'thomas'	'LPT3'	'Third floor's printer'
NULL	'LPT4'	'Common printer for new user'
NULL	'LPT5'	'Common printer for new user'

When 'chacha' executes the report, he is entitled to use only LPT1, whereas a user named 'celko' is expected to use either LPT4 or LPT5. In the first case, a simple query can pull out one row and it works fine; in the second case, you get two rows and cannot use that result. Can you come up with a one-query solution?

Answer

I would answer that the problem is in the data. Look at the userid column. The name tells you that it should be unique, but it has multiple NULLs in it. There is also another problem in the real world: you want to balance the printer loads between LPT4 and LPT5, so that one of them is not overused.

Don't write a fancy query; change the table:

```
CREATE TABLE PrinterControl
(userid_start CHAR(8) NOT NULL,
 userid_finish CHAR(8) NOT NULL,
 printer_name CHAR(4) NOT NULL,
 description CHAR(40) NOT NULL,
 PRIMARY KEY (userid_start, userid_finish));
```

Now consider the following example:

PrinterControl

userid_start	userid_finish	printer_name	description
'chacha'	'chacha'	'LPT1'	'First floor's printer'
'lee'	'lee'	'LPT2'	'Second floor's printer'
'thomas'	'thomas'	'LPT3'	'Third floor's printer'
'aaaaaaaa'	'mzzzzzzz'	'LPT4'	'Common printer #1'
'naaaaaaa'	'zzzzzzzz'	'LPT5'	'Common printer #2'

The query then becomes

```
SELECT MIN(printer_name)
  FROM PrinterControl
 WHERE :my_id BETWEEN userid_start AND userid_finish;
```

The trick is in the start and finish values, which partition the range of possible strings between 'aaa...' and 'zzz...' any way you wish. The 'celko' user id qualified only for LPT4, because it falls alphabetically within that range of strings. A user 'norman' is qualified only for LPT5. Careful choice of these ranges will allow you to distribute the printer loads evenly if you know what the user ids are going to be like.

I have also made an assumption that the common printers will always have higher LPT numbers. When 'chacha' goes to this table, he will get a result set of (LPT1, LPT4), and then pick the minimum value, LPT1, from it. A smart optimizer should be able to use the PRIMARY KEY index to speed up the query.

AVAILABLE SEATS

You have a restaurant with 1,000 seats. Whenever a waiter puts
someone in a seat, he logs it in a table of seats (I was going to say
"table of tables" and make this impossible to read). Likewise, when a
guest finishes a meal, you remove that guest's seat number. You want
to write a query to produce a list of the available seats in the restaurant. Oh, yes, the gimmick is that the database resides on a personal
digital assistant and not a mainframe computer. You must do this
with the smallest amount of storage possible. Assume each seat number is an integer.

The first thought is to add a (free/occupied) flag column next to
the seat-number column. The available-seating query would be based
on the flag. This would be 1,000 rows of one integer and one character for the whole restaurant and would work pretty well, but we have
that minimal-storage requirement. Darn!

Answer #1

The flag can be represented by a plus or minus on the seat number
itself to save the extra column, but this is very bad relational practice; two attributes are being collapsed into one column. However, it
does keep us at 1,000 rows.

Answer #2

The second thought is to create a second table with a single column
of occupied seating and to move numbers between the occupied and
available tables. That would require a total of 1,000 rows in both tables.

Answer #3

Instead, we can use a single table and create seats 0 through 1001 (0
and 1001 do not really exist and are never assigned to a customer).
Delete each seat from the table as it is occupied and insert it back
when it is free again The Restaurant table can get as small as the

two dummy rows if all the seating is taken, but no bigger than 1002 rows (2004 bytes) if the house is empty.

This VIEW will find the first seat in a gap of open seats:

```
CREATE VIEW Firstseat (seat)
    AS SELECT (seat + 1)
        FROM Restaurant
        WHERE (seat + 1) NOT IN
        (SELECT seat FROM Restaurant)
        AND (seat + 1) < 1001;
```

Likewise, this VIEW finds the last seat in a gap of open seats:

```
CREATE VIEW Lastseat (seat)
    AS SELECT (seat - 1)
        FROM Restaurant
        WHERE (seat - 1) NOT IN
        (SELECT seat FROM Restaurant)
        AND (seat - 1) > 0;
```

Now use these two VIEWs to show the blocks of empty seats:

```
SELECT F1.seat AS start, L1.seat AS finish,
            ((L1.seat - F1.seat) + 1) AS available
  FROM Firstseat AS F1, Lastseat AS L1
 WHERE L1.seat = (SELECT MIN(L2.seat)
                    FROM Lastseat AS L2
                    WHERE F1.seat <= L2.seat);
```

This query will also tell you how many available seats are in each block, a fact that could be handy for a waiter to know when seating groups. It is left as an exercise for the reader to write this as a single query without VIEWs.

10 WAGES OF SIN

Luke Tymowski, a Canadian programmer, posted an interesting problem on the MS-ACCESS Forum on CompuServe in November 1994. He was working on a pension fund problem. In SQL-92, the table involved would look like this:

```
CREATE TABLE Pensions
(sin CHAR(10) NOT NULL,
 penyear INTEGER NOT NULL,
 service INTEGER NOT NULL DEFAULT 0
     CHECK (service BETWEEN 0 AND 12),
 earnings DECIMAL (8,2) NOT NULL DEFAULT 0.00);
```

The SIN column is the Social Insurance Number, which is something like the SSN (Social Security Number) used in the United States to identify taxpayers. The penyear column is the calendar year of the pension, the service column is the number of months the person worked in that year, and earnings is the person's total earnings for that year.

The problem is to find the total earnings of each employee for the most recent 60 months of service in consecutive years. This number is used to compute the employee's pension. The shortest period, going back, could be 5 years with 12 months of service in each. The longest period could be 60 years with 1 month of service in each. Some people might work four years and not the fifth, and thus not qualify for a pension at all.

The reason this is a beast to solve is that "most recent" and "consecutive" are hard to write in SQL.

HINT: *For each employee in each year, insert a row even in the years that employee did not work. Not only does it make the query easier, but you also have a record to update when you get in new information.*

Answer #1

This query will get me the starting and ending years of consecutive periods in which (1) the employee worked (i.e., service greater than 0 months) and (2) the service totaled 60 or more months.

```
CREATE VIEW PenPeriods (sin, startyr, endyr, tot_earnings)
AS SELECT P0.sin, P0.penyear, P1.penyear,
  (SELECT SUM (earnings) -- total earnings for period
    FROM Pensions AS P2
   WHERE P2.sin = P0.sin
     AND P2.penyear BETWEEN P0.penyear AND P1.penyear)
   FROM Pensions AS P0, Pensions AS P1
   WHERE P1.sin = P0.sin    -- self-join to make intervals
     AND P1.penyear >= (P0.penyear - 4) -- why sooner?
     AND 0 < ALL (SELECT service  -- consecutive service
                  FROM Pensions AS P3
                  WHERE P3.sin = P0.sin
                    AND P3.penyear
                    BETWEEN P0.penyear AND P1.penyear)
     AND 60 <= (SELECT SUM (service) -- total more than 60
                  FROM Pensions AS P4
                  WHERE P4.sin = P0.sin
                    AND P4.penyear
                    BETWEEN P0.penyear AND P1.penyear);
```

The subquery expression in the SELECT list is an SQL-92 trick, but a number of products already have it.

The gimmick is that this will give you *all* the periods of 60 months or more. What we really want is the most recent endyr. I would handle this with the Pension Period VIEW I just defined and a MAX(endyr) predicate:

```
SELECT *
  FROM PenPeriods AS P0
 WHERE endyr = (SELECT MAX(endyr)
                FROM PenPeriods AS P1
                WHERE P1.sin = P0.sin);
```

I can handle that with some ugly HAVING clauses in SQL-92, I could combine both those subquery predicates with an EXISTS() clause, and so on. The trouble is that these features would not be as portable right now.

As an exercise, you can try to add another predicate to the final subquery that says there does not exist a year between P0.penyear and P1.penyear that is greater than the P4.penyear and still gives a total of 60 or more consecutive months.

Answer #2

Most of the improved solutions I got via CompuServe were based on my original answer. However, Richard Romley sent in the best one and used a completely different approach. Here's his answer:

```
SELECT Beg.sin,
       Beg.penyear AS startyear,
       Fini.penyear AS endyear,
       SUM (Mid.earnings)
  FROM Pensions AS Beg, Pensions AS Mid, Pensions AS Fini
 WHERE Beg.service > 0
   AND Mid.service > 0
   AND Fini.service > 0
   AND Beg.sin = Mid.sin
   AND Beg.sin = Fini.sin
   AND Beg.penyear BETWEEN Fini.penyear-59 AND (Fini.penyear - 4)
   AND Mid.penyear BETWEEN Beg.penyear AND Fini.penyear
 GROUP BY Beg.sin, Beg.penyear, Fini.penyear
HAVING SUM (Mid.service) >= 60
   AND (Fini.penyear - Beg.penyear) = (COUNT (*) - 1);
```

Mr. Romley wrote, "This problem would have been easier if there were no rows allowed with (service = 0). I had to waste three WHERE clauses just to filter them out!" Another example of how a better data design would have made life easier.

The outstanding parts of this answer are the use of the BETWEEN predicate to look at durations in the range of 5 to 60 years (the minimum and maximum time needed to acquire 60 months of service) and the use of grouping columns in the last expression in the HAVING clause to guarantee consecutive years.

When I ran this query on WATCOM SQL 4.0, the query planner estimate was four times greater for Mr. Romley's solution than for my original solution, but his *actually* runs faster. I would guess that the plan estimation is being fooled by the three-way self-joins, which are usually very expensive.

PUZZLE

11 WORK ORDER

Cenk Ersoy asked this question on the Gupta Forum on
CompuServe. He has a table that looks like this:

```
CREATE TABLE Projects
(workorder CHAR(5) NOT NULL,
 leg INTEGER NOT NULL CHECK (leg BETWEEN 0 AND 1000),
 status CHAR(1) NOT NULL CHECK (status IN ('C', 'R'));
```

Also some sample data like this:

Projects

workorder	leg	status
'AA100'	0	'C'
'AA100'	1	'R'
'AA100'	2	'R'
'AA200'	0	'R'
'AA200'	1	'R'
'AA300'	0	'C'
'AA300'	1	'C'

He would like to get the work orders for which the leg is zero
and the status is 'C', but all other legs for that work order have a status of 'R'. For example, the query should return only 'AA100' in the
sample data.

Answer

This is really fairly straightforward, but you have to reword the
query specification in the passive voice to see the answer. Instead of
saying "all other legs for that work order have a status of 'R'," instead
say "'R' is the status of all the nonzero legs" and the answer falls out
immediately, thus:

```
SELECT workorder
  FROM Projects AS P1
 WHERE leg = 0
   AND status = 'C'
   AND 'R' = ALL (SELECT status
                    FROM Projects AS P2
                   WHERE leg <> 0
                     AND P1.workorder = P2.workorder);
```

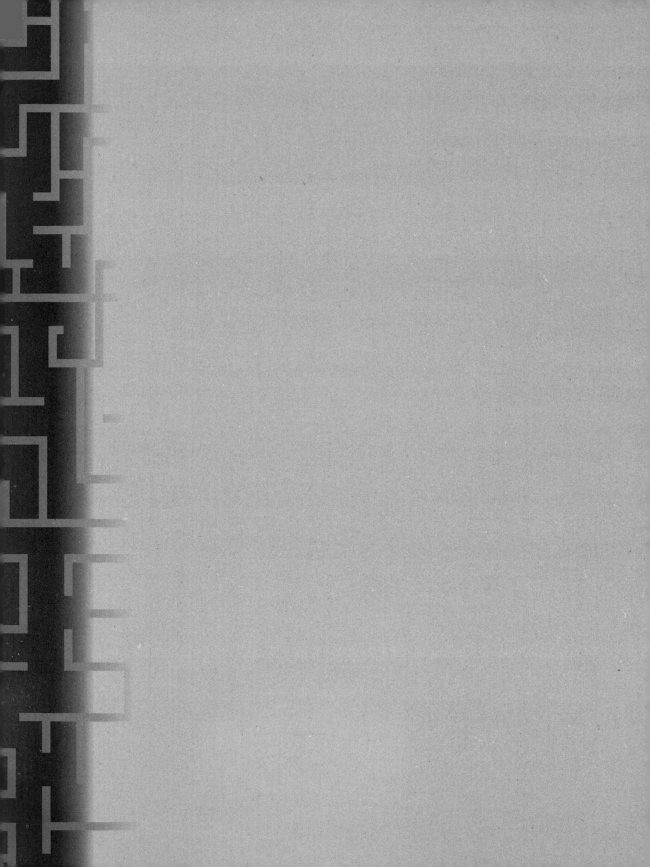

CHAPTER

2

Formatting Data

WE USED TO joke that "SQL" stands for "Scarcely Qualifies as a Language," because it is strictly a database language. The only input statement in ANSI/ISO Standard SQL is INSERT INTO and there is no output statement per se. The query results are passed to the host program via a cursor and the host program worries about handling displays.

You can CAST() values from one datatype to another and perform some limited string operations, but you cannot control the display format of the data as you can in traditional programming languages such as Cobol, Fortran, PL/I, BASIC, and so forth. SQL simply has nothing like Cobol's PICTURE, Fortran's FORMAT, or PL/I's PUT EDIT.

You will find products that use functions that convert the internal datatype into formatted strings, but this is not part of the ANSI/ISO standard. If you wanted to imitate a Fortran FORMAT or a Cobol PICTURE statement in Standard SQL, you would have to use a lot of calls to CAST(), SUBSTRING(), concatenation, and other string functions.

But it is nice if you can hand the host language a result table whose rows look as if they were coming off of a sequential file that was exactly designed for their problem. The host language can then do its display work with minimal effort. This is what I mean by formatting in SQL.

PUZZLE

12 CLAIMS STATUS

Leonard C. Medal posted this problem on CompuServe in November 1995. Patients make legal claims against a medical institution and we record it in the Claims table:

Claims

claimid	patient
10	'Smith'
20	'Jones'
30	'Brown'

Each claim has one or more defendants, usually physicians, recorded in the table 'Claimdefendant':

Claimdefendant

claimid	defendant
10	'Johnson'
10	'Meyer'
10	'Dow'
20	'Baker'
20	'Meyer'
30	'Johnson'

Each defendant associated with a claim has a history of events, in which changes in the status of the defendant on a given claim are recorded:

Events

claimid	defendant	status	changedate
10	'Johnson'	'AP'	'1994-01-01'
10	'Johnson'	'OR'	'1994-02-01'
10	'Johnson'	'SF'	'1994-03-01'
10	'Johnson'	'CL'	'1994-04-01'

(cont.)

claimid	defendant	status	changedate
10	'Meyer'	'AP'	'1994-01-01'
10	'Meyer'	'OR'	'1994-02-01'
10	'Meyer'	'SF'	'1994-03-01'
10	'Dow'	'AP'	'1994-01-01'
10	'Dow'	'OR'	'1994-02-01'
20	'Meyer'	'AP'	'1994-01-01'
20	'Meyer'	'OR'	'1994-02-01'
20	'Baker'	'AP'	'1994-01-01'
30	'Johnson'	'AP'	'1994-01-01'

Changes in status for each defendant occur in a known sequence, determined by law, as shown in the Status table:

StatusCodes

status	statusdesc	seq
'AP'	'Awaiting review panel'	1
'OR'	'Panel opinion rendered'	2
'SF'	'Suit filed'	3
'CL'	'Closed'	4

The status of a defendant (with regard to a given claim) is his/her latest status, which is the status with the highest sequence number. For certain legal reasons, events ordered by date do not always correspond to events ordered by sequence number.

The status of a claim is the status of the defendant who has the lowest status of all the defendants involved in the claim. This makes the claim status a minimum of the maximums. For this sample data, the answer would be

claimid	patient	status
10	'Smith'	'OR'
20	'Jones'	'AP'
30	'Brown'	'AP'

The problem is to find the status of each claim and display it. I counted this as a display problem.

Answer #1

Mr. Medal's answer was a single SQL query that directly translated the description into code:

```
SELECT C1.claimid, C1.patient, T2.status
  FROM Claims AS C1, StatusCodes AS T2
 WHERE T2.seq
       IN (SELECT MIN(S2.seq)
             FROM StatusCodes AS S2
            WHERE S2.seq
                  IN (SELECT MAX(S3.seq)
                        FROM Events AS E1, StatusCodes AS S3
                       WHERE E1.status = S3.status
                         AND E1.claimid = C1.claimid
                       GROUP BY E1.defendant));
```

Answer #2

But there is another solution. It is easier to get the set of all status codes within a claim that all the defendants have obtained:

```
SELECT E1.claimid, C1.patient, E1.status
  FROM Events AS E1, Claims AS C1
 WHERE E1.claimid = C1.claimid
 GROUP BY E1.claimid, C1.patient, E1.status
HAVING COUNT(*) = (SELECT COUNT(DISTINCT defendant)
                     FROM Events AS E2
                    WHERE E1.claimid = E2.claimid)
 ORDER BY E1.claimid;
```

But, more to the point, look at the StatusCodes table and you will see that status and seq are both keys that point to the status description (actually, all three columns are keys). This is a code translation table.

If we dropped the two-letter status code domain and replaced it with the numeric seq in all the places where it occurs, we would get a result from which we could easily pick the maximum value of the seq column in each claim. A quick way to do this translation is with a scalar subquery in the SELECT clause:

```
SELECT E1.claimid, C1.patient, (SELECT seq
                                  FROM StatusCodes AS S1
                                 WHERE S1.status = E1.status)
  FROM Events AS E1, Claims AS C1
 WHERE E1.claimid = C1.claimid
 GROUP BY E1.claimid, C1.patient, E1.status
HAVING COUNT(*) = (SELECT COUNT(DISTINCT defendant)
                     FROM Events AS E2
                    WHERE E1.claimid = E2.claimid)
 ORDER BY E1.claimid;
```

Answer #3

Sorin Shtirbu submitted a third answer:

```
SELECT claimid, MAX(patient), MAX(T1.status)
  FROM Status AS T1, Claims AS C1
 WHERE T1.seq =
       (SELECT MAX(T2.seq)
          FROM Status AS T2, Events AS E1
         WHERE T2.status = E1.status
           AND E1.claimid = C1.claimid
         GROUP BY E1.claimid, defendant)
 GROUP BY claimid, T1.seq
 HAVING T1.seq = MIN(T1.seq);
```

It is a good question if this third approach is more efficient or not. It might depend on indexing and how the implementation handles subquery versus a GROUP BY.

PUZZLE

13 TEACHER

Brendan Campbell posted an interesting problem on the Oracle User Group Forum on CompuServe in May 1996. He gave me permission to use it and to publish his alternative PL/SQL solution as a bad example, thus submitting himself to public humiliation and disgrace for the good of science. Donating your body is easy—you're dead—but donating your dignity is hard.

We want a query to pass to a report program that shows the names of the instructors for each course and each student. Now here's the catch: we physically have room for only two instructor names on the printout.

If there is only one instructor, display the instructor's name in the first instructor column and set the second column to blanks or NULL. If there are exactly two instructors, display both names in ascending order. If there are more than two instructors, the report will display the name of the first instructor in the first column and the string '--More--' in the second instructor column.

Assume the necessary data is in a table like this:

```
CREATE TABLE Register
(course INTEGER NOT NULL,
student CHAR(10) NOT NULL,
instructor CHAR(10) NOT NULL,
```

Brendan's original solution was 70 lines long; the pure SQL answer is about 12 lines of code in a single statement.

Answer #1

One method is to use the extrema functions.

```
SELECT R1.course, R1.student, MIN(R1.instructor), NULL
  FROM Register AS R1
 GROUP BY R1.course, R1.student
```

```
HAVING COUNT(*) = 1
UNION
SELECT R1.course, R1.student, MIN(R1.instructor),
       MAX(R1.instructor)
  FROM Register AS R1
 GROUP BY R1.course, R1.student
HAVING COUNT(*) = 2
UNION
SELECT R1.course, R1.student, MIN(R1.instructor), '--More--'
  FROM Register AS R1
 GROUP BY R1.course, R1.student
HAVING COUNT(*) > 2;
```

Now, to go into my usual painful details:

The first SELECT statement picks the course/student combinations with one and only one instructor. See why the MIN() works? Without any competition, the only instructor will be the minimum by default. I like to use NULLs for missing values, but you could use a string constant instead.

The second SELECT statement picks the course/student combinations with two and only two instructors. The MIN() and MAX() functions work and order the names because there are only two instructors.

The third SELECT statement picks the course/student combinations with more than two instructors. I use the MIN() to get the first instructor, then a constant of 'more', as per the report specification, in the second column.

Answer #2

Richard S. Romley once more cooked my published solution by collapsing the two SELECT statements into a CASE expression with the extrema functions in SQL-92 syntax, like this:

```
SELECT course, student, MIN(instructor),
       CASE COUNT(*) WHEN 1 THEN NULL
                     WHEN 2 THEN MAX(instructor)
                     ELSE '--More--'
```

```
FROM Register
GROUP BY course, student;
```

This version of the CASE expression might have problems in existing implementations. Some older SQL products do not implement a CASE expression at all; others do not allow aggregate functions in it. This version of the CASE expression can also be replaced with another syntax, which is equivalent:

```
CASE WHEN COUNT(*) = 1 THEN NULL
     WHEN COUNT(*) = 2 THEN MAX(instructor)
     ELSE '--More--'
```

You'll find that a CASE expression in the SELECT list is very handy for display problems.

14 TELEPHONE

Suppose you're trying to set up an office telephone directory with your new database-publishing system, and you have the following tables:

```
CREATE TABLE Employees
(empid INTEGER PRIMARY KEY,
 firstname CHAR(20) NOT NULL,
 lastname CHAR(20) NOT NULL);


CREATE TABLE Phones
(empid INTEGER NOT NULL,
 phonetype CHAR(3) NOT NULL
        CHECK (phonetype IN (('hom', 'fax'))),
 phonenumber CHAR(12) NOT NULL,
 PRIMARY KEY (empid, phonetype, phonenumber),
 FOREIGN KEY empid REFERENCES Employees.empid);
```

The codes 'hom' and 'fax' indicate whether the number is the employee's home phone number or a fax number. You want to print out a report with one line per employee that gives both numbers if it has them and shows a NULL if either or both numbers are missing.

I should note here that the FOREIGN KEY constraint on the Phones table means that you cannot list a telephone number for someone who is not an employee. The PRIMARY KEY looks a bit large until you stop and think about all the cases. Married employees could share the same fax or home telephones, or a single line could be used for both voice and fax services.

Answer

You can do a lot of things wrong with this query. The first thought is to construct the home telephone information as a query in its own right. Because you want to see all the employees, you need an OUTER JOIN:

```
CREATE VIEW Hphones (lastname, firstname, empid, homenumber)
AS SELECT E1.lastname, E1.firstname, E1.empid, H1.phonenumber
     FROM (Employees AS E1
            LEFT OUTER JOIN
            Phones AS H1
            ON E1.empid = H1.empid AND H1.phonetype = 'hom');
```

Likewise, you could construct the fax information as a query, using the same approach:

```
CREATE VIEW Fphones (lastname, firstname, empid, faxnumber)
AS SELECT E1.lastname, E1.empid, F1.phonenumber
     FROM (Employees AS E1
            LEFT OUTER JOIN
            Phones AS F1
            ON E1.empid = F1.empid AND F1.phonetype = 'fax');
```

It would seem reasonable to combine these two VIEWs to get

```
SELECT Hphones.lastname, Hphones.firstname, homenumber, faxnumber
  FROM Hphones AS H1, Fphones AS F1
  WHERE H1.empid = F1.empid;
```

But this does not work, because it leaves out the "fax-only" people. If you want to preserve both phone tables, you need a FULL OUTER JOIN, which might look like this:

```
SELECT H1.lastname, H1.firstname, homenumber, faxnumber
  FROM Hphones AS H1
        FULL OUTER JOIN
        Fphones AS F1
        ON H1.empid = F1.empid;
```

But this still does not print the names of the "fax-only" people who show up as NULLs, because you're printing only the Hphones people's names. The COALESCE() function will take care of that problem for you. It will take a list of expressions and return the first non-NULL value that it finds, reading from left to right:

```
SELECT COALESCE (H1.lastname, F1.lastname),
       COALESCE (H1.firstname, F1.firstname),
       homenumber, faxnumber
  FROM Hphones AS H1
       FULL OUTER JOIN
       Fphones AS F1
       ON H1.empid = F1.empid;
```

The bad news is that this will work but it will run like glue, because it will probably materialize the VIEWs before using them. The real trick is to go back and see that the Fphones and Hphones VIEWs are OUTER JOINed to the Employees table. You can factor out the Employees table and combine the two FROM clauses to give

```
SELECT E1.lastname, E1.firstname,
       H1.phonenumber AS Home,
       F1.phonenumber AS FAX
  FROM (Employees AS E1
        LEFT OUTER JOIN
        Phones AS H1
        ON E1.empid = H1.empid AND H1.phonetype = 'hom)
        LEFT OUTER JOIN
        Phones AS F1
        ON E1.empid = F1.empid AND F1.phonetype = 'fax';
```

Because this gets all the tables at once, it should run a good bit faster than the false start. This is also a query that you cannot write easily using Sybase-, Oracle-, or Gupta-style extended equality OUTER JOIN syntax, because such a syntax cannot handle nesting of OUTER JOINs.

PUZZLE
15 FIND THE LAST TWO SALARIES

Jack Wells sent this perplexing SQL problem in June 1996 over CompuServe. His situation is pretty typical for SQL programmers who have to work with 3GL people. The programmers are writing a report on the employees, and they want to get information about each employee's current and previous salary status so they can produce a report. The report needs to show the date of each person's promotion and the salary amount.

This is pretty easy if you can put each salary in one row in the result set and let the host program format it. That is the first programming problem for the reader, in fact.

Oh, I forgot to mention that the application programmers are a bunch of lazy bums and want to have both the current and the previous salary information on one row for each employee. This will let them write a very simple cursor statement and print out the report without any real work on their part.

Jack spoke with Fabian Pascal, author of *Understanding Relational Databases* (John Wiley, 1993, ISBN 0-471-58538-6) and *SQL and Relational Basics* (M&T Books, 1989, ISBN 1-55851-063-X), the week he was working on this problem and Mr. Pascal said this query could not be done. He said, "In a truly relational language it could be done, but since SQL is not relational it isn't possible, not even with SQL-92." Sounds like a challenge to me!

Oh, I forgot to mention an additional constraint on the query; Jack is working in Oracle. This product is still not up to SQL-92 standards (i.e., no proper OUTER JOINs, no general scalar subexpressions, and so on), so his query has to run under the old SQL-89 rules.

Assume that we have this test data:

```
CREATE TABLE Salaries
(emp CHAR(10) NOT NULL,
 sal_date DATE NOT NULL,
 sal_amt DECIMAL (8,2) NOT NULL,
 PRIMARY KEY (emp, sal_date));
```

```
INSERT INTO Salaries
VALUES (('Tom', '1996-06-20', 500.00),
        ('Tom', '1996-08-20', 700.00),
        ('Tom', '1996-10-20', 800.00),
        ('Tom', '1996-12-20', 900.00),
        ('Dick', '1996-06-20', 500.00),
        ('Harry', '1996-07-20', 500.00),
        ('Harry', '1996-09-20', 700.00));
```

Tom has had two promotions, Dick is a new hire, and Harry has had one promotion.

Answer #1

First let's do the easy problem. The answer is to use the query I call a generalized extrema or "top (n)" function and put it in a VIEW, like this:

```
CREATE VIEW Salaries1 (empno, curr_sal_date, curr_sal_amt)
AS SELECT S0.empno, S0.sal_date, MAX(S0.sal_amt)
     FROM Salaries AS S0, Salaries AS S1
    WHERE S0.sal_date >= S1.sal_date
    GROUP BY S0.empno, S0.sal_date
   HAVING COUNT(*) <= 2;


CREATE VIEW Salaries2 (emp, sal_date, sal_amt)
AS SELECT S0.emp, S0.sal_date, MAX(S0.sal_amt)
     FROM Salaries AS S0, Salaries AS S1
    WHERE S0.sal_date <= S1.sal_date
      AND S0.emp = S1.emp
    GROUP BY S0.emp, S0.sal_date
   HAVING COUNT(*) <= 2;
```

Results

emp	sal_date	sal_amt
'Dick'	'1996-06-20'	500.00
'Harry'	'1996-07-20'	500.00
'Harry'	'1996-09-20'	700.00
'Tom'	'1996-10-20'	800.00
'Tom'	'1996-12-20'	900.00

The S1 copy of the Salaries table determines the boundary of the subset of two or fewer salary changes for each employee. The MAX( ) function is a trick to get the salary amount column in the results. This gives you one row for each of the first two salary changes for each employee. If the programmers were not so lazy, you could pass this table to them and let them format it for the report.

Answer #2

The real problem is harder. One way to do this within the limits of SQL-89 is to break the problem into two cases:

1. Employees with only one salary action.

2. Employees with two or more salary actions.

We know that every employee has to fall into one and only one of those cases. One solution is to UNION both of the sets together:

```
SELECT S0.emp, S0.sal_date, S0.sal_amt, S1.sal_date, S1.sal_amt
  FROM Salaries AS S0, Salaries AS S1
 WHERE S0.emp = S1.emp
 AND S0.sal_date =
     (SELECT MAX(S2.sal_date)
        FROM Salaries AS S2
       WHERE S0.emp = S2.emp)
```

```
AND S1.sal_date =
   (SELECT MAX(S3.sal_date)
      FROM Salaries AS S3
     WHERE S0.emp = S3.emp
       AND S3.sal_date < S0.sal_date)
UNION ALL
SELECT S4.emp, MAX(S4.sal_date), MAX(S4.sal_amt), NULL, NULL
  FROM Salaries AS S4
 GROUP BY S4.emp
HAVING COUNT(*) = 1;
```

emp	sal_date	sal_amt	sal_date	sal_amt
'Tom'	'1996-12-20'	900.00	'1996-10-20'	800.00
'Harry'	'1996-09-20'	700.00	'1996-07-20'	500.00
'Dick'	'1996-06-20'	500.00	NULL	NULL

DB2 programmers will recognize this as a version of the OUTER JOIN done without an SQL-92 standard OUTER JOIN operator. The first SELECT statement is the hardest. It is a self-join on the Salaries table, with copy S0 as the source for the most recent salary information and copy S1 as the source for the next most recent information. The second SELECT statement is simply a grouped query that locates the employees with one row. Since the two result sets are disjoint, we can use the UNION ALL instead of a UNION operator to save an extra sorting operation.

Answer #3

I got several answers in response to my challenge for a better solution to this puzzle. Richard Romley of Smith Barney sent in the following SQL-92 solution. It takes advantage of the subquery table expression to avoid VIEWs:

```
SELECT B.emp, B.maxdate, Y.sal_amt, B.maxdate2, Z.sal_amt
  FROM (SELECT A.emp, A.maxdate, maxdate2 = MAX(X.sal_date)
          FROM (SELECT W.emp, maxdate = MAX(W.sal_date)
                  FROM Salaries AS W
                 GROUP BY W.emp) AS A
```

```
LEFT OUTER JOIN Salaries AS X
  ON A.emp = X.emp
    AND A.maxdate > X.sal_date
  GROUP BY A.emp, A.maxdate) AS B
LEFT OUTER JOIN Salaries AS Y
  ON B.emp = Y.emp
    AND B.maxdate = Y.sal_date
LEFT OUTER JOIN Salaries AS Z
  ON B.emp = Z.emp
    AND B.maxdate2 = Z.sal_date;
```

If your SQL product does not support anything but a TABLE or
VIEW name in the OUTER JOINs, you can convert some of the subqueries into VIEWs for the table subqueries named A and B.

Answer #4

Mike Conway came up with an answer in Oracle, which I tried to
translate into SQL-92 with mixed results. The problem with the
translation was that the Oracle version of SQL does not support the
SQL-92 standard OUTER JOIN syntax and you have to watch the
order of execution to get the right results. Syed Kadir, an associate
application engineer at Oracle, sent in an improvement on my
answer, using the VIEW that was created in the first solution:

```
SELECT S1.emp, S1.sal_date, S1.sal_amt, S2.sal_date, S2.sal_amt
  FROM Salaries1 AS S1, Salaries2 AS S2  -- use the view
 WHERE S1.emp = S2.emp
   AND S1.sal_date > S2.sal_date
UNION ALL
SELECT emp, MAX(sal_date), MAX(sal_amt), NULL, NULL
  FROM Salaries1
 GROUP BY emp
HAVING COUNT(*) = 1;
```

You might have to replace the last two columns with the expressions CAST(NULL AS DATE) and CAST(NULL AS DECIMAL(8,2)) to
ensure that they are of the right datatypes for a UNION.

Answer #5

Richard Romley and I went back and forth via email about other possible solutions until we both came up with an unorthodox approach, which I wanted to reject on artistic grounds. But in the end, performance is the ultimate judge.

The trick is to convert the dates and salaries into strings, concatenate them with the date string first, and then split the salary back out.

```
SELECT A.emp,
       MAX(A.sal_date) AS date1,
       SUBSTRING (MAX(CAST(A.sal_date AS CHAR(10))
            || CAST(A.sal_amt AS CHAR(8))), 11, 8) AS sal1,

       MAX(B.sal_date) AS date2,
       SUBSTRING (MAX(CAST(B.sal_date AS CHAR(10))
            || CAST(B.sal_amt AS CHAR(8))), 11, 8) AS sal2
  FROM Salaries AS A
       LEFT OUTER JOIN
       Salaries AS B
       ON A.emp = B.emp
          AND A.sal_date > B.sal_date
 GROUP BY A.emp;
```

If you wanted to, you could also CAST() the whole substring expression back to DECIMAL(8,2) so you would have the original datatype. Another advantage is that this pattern can be extended by adding more MAX() and SUBSTRING() pairs with matching LEFT OUTER JOINs.

CHAPTER

3

Selecting Data

I TELL MY SQL classes that the language is very easy to learn because the SELECT ... FROM ... statement does 90% of your work. Learn just one statement and you have a firm grasp of this new programming language! Of course, this is like saying LISP is easy because every program is only one function call.

The gimmick, of course, is that a single SELECT statement can be as nested, convoluted, and complex as any procedural-language program.

The following puzzles depend on finding a neat way to pick a subset of the tables in the schema that may not be obvious at first.

16 MECHANICS

Gerard Manko, at ARI, posted this problem on CompuServe in April 1994. ARI had just switched over from Paradox to WATCOM SQL (now called Sybase SQL Anywhere). The conversion of the legacy database was done by making each Paradox table into a Sybase SQL Anywhere table, without any thought of normalization or integrity rules—just copy the column names and datatypes. Yes, I know that as the SQL guru, I should have sent him to that circle of hell reserved for people who do not normalize. But that does not get the job done, and ARI's approach is something I find in the real world all the time.

The system tracks teams of employees to work on jobs. Each job has a slot for a single primary mechanic and a slot for a single optional assistant mechanic. The tables involved look like this:

```
CREATE TABLE Jobs
(jobid INTEGER NOT NULL PRIMARY KEY,
 startdate DATE NOT NULL,
 ... );

CREATE TABLE Employees
(empid INTEGER NOT NULL PRIMARY KEY,
 name CHAR (20) NOT NULL,
 ... );

CREATE TABLE Teams
(jobid INTEGER NOT NULL,
 mechtype INTEGER NOT NULL,
 empid INTEGER NOT NULL,
 ... );
```

Your first task is to add some integrity checking into the Teams table. Do not worry about normalization or the other tables for this problem.

What you want to do is build a query for a report that lists all the jobs by jobid, the primary mechanic (if any), and the assistant mechanic (if any). Here are some hints: You can get the jobids from Jobs because that table has all the current jobs, while the Teams table lists only those jobs for which a team has been assigned. The same person can be assigned as both a primary and an assistant mechanic on the same job.

Answer #1

The first problem is to add referential integrity. The Teams table should probably be tied to the others with FOREIGN KEY references, and it is always a good idea to check the codes in the database schema, as follows:

```
CREATE TABLE Teams
(jobid INTEGER NOT NULL REFERENCES Jobs(jobid),
 mechtype CHAR(10) NOT NULL
      CHECK (mechtype IN ('Primary', 'Assistant')),
 empid INTEGER NOT NULL REFERENCES Employees(empid),
     ...);
```

Experienced SQL people will immediately think of using a LEFT OUTER JOIN, because to get the primary mechanics only, you could write

```
SELECT Jobs.jobid, Teams.empid AS "Primary",
 FROM Jobs LEFT OUTER JOIN Teams
         ON Jobs.jobid = Teams.jobid
 WHERE Teams.mechtype = 'Primary';
```

You can do a similar OUTER JOIN to the Employees table to tie it to Teams. But the problem here is that you want to do two independent OUTER JOINs for each mechanic's slot on a team and put the results in one table. It is probably possible to build a horrible, deeply nested self OUTER JOIN all in one SELECT statement, but you would not be able to read or understand it. You could do the report with views for primary and assistant mechanics and then put them together. But you can avoid all of this mess with the following query:

```
SELECT Jobs.jobid,
    (SELECT empid
       FROM Teams
      WHERE Jobs.jobid = Teams.jobid
        AND Teams.mechtype = 'Primary') AS "Primary",
    (SELECT empid
       FROM Teams
      WHERE Jobs.jobid = Teams.jobid
        AND Teams.mechtype = 'Assistant') AS Assistant
  FROM Jobs;
```

The reason that "Primary" is in double quotation marks is that it is a reserved word in SQL-92, as in PRIMARY KEY. The double quotation marks make the word into an identifier. When the same word appears in single quotation marks, it is treated as a character string.

The trick is the ability to use two independent scalar SELECT statements in the outermost SELECT. To add the employee's name, simply change the innermost SELECT statements.

```
SELECT Jobs.jobid,
      (SELECT name
         FROM Teams, Employees
        WHERE Jobs.jobid = Teams.jobid
          AND Employees.empid = Teams.empid
          AND Teams.mechtype = 'Primary') AS "Primary",
      (SELECT name
         FROM Teams, Employees
        WHERE Jobs.jobid = Teams.jobid
          AND Employees.empid = Teams.empid
          AND Teams.mechtype = 'Assistant') AS Assistant
  FROM Jobs:
```

If you have an employee acting as both primary and assistant mechanic on a single job, you'll get that employee in both slots. If you have two or more primary mechanics or two or more assistant mechanics on a job, you'll get an error, as you should. If you have no primary or assistant mechanic, you'll get an empty SELECT result, which becomes a NULL. That gives you the OUTER JOINs you wanted.

Answer #2

Skip Lees, of Chico, California, wanted to make the Teams table enforce these rules:

1. A jobid has zero or one primary mechanics.

2. A jobid has zero or one assistant mechanics.

3. A jobid always has at least one mechanic of some kind.

Based on rule 3, there should be no time at which a job has no team members. Therefore, team information will have to be entered before job records. Using a referential integrity constraint will enforce this constraint. Restrictions 1 and 2 can be enforced by making "jobid" and "mechtype" into a two-column PRIMARY KEY, so that a jobid could never be entered more than once with a given mechtype.

```
CREATE TABLE Jobs
(jobid INTEGER NOT NULL PRIMARY KEY REFERENCES Teams (jobid),
 startdate DATE NOT NULL,
 ... );
```

```
CREATE TABLE Teams
(jobid INTEGER NOT NULL,
mechtype CHAR(10) NOT NULL
 CHECK (mechtype IN ('Primary', 'Assistant')),
empid INTEGER NOT NULL REFERENCE Employees(empid),
 ...
PRIMARY KEY (jobid, mechtype));
```

There is a subtle "gotcha" in this problem. SQL-92 says that a REFERENCES clause in the referencing table has to reference a

UNIQUE or PRIMARY KEY column set in the referenced table. That is, the reference is to be to the same number of columns, of the same datatypes in the same order, since we have a PRIMARY KEY (jobid, mechtype) available in the Teams table in your answer. Therefore, the jobid column in the Jobs table by itself cannot reference just the jobid column in the Teams table. You could get around this with a UNIQUE constraint:

```
CREATE TABLE Teams
(jobid INTEGER NOT NULL UNIQUE,
 mechtype CHAR(10) NOT NULL
 CHECK (mechtype IN ('Primary', 'Assistant')),
 PRIMARY KEY (jobid, mechtype));
```

but it might be more natural to say

```
CREATE TABLE Teams
(jobid INTEGER NOT NULL PRIMARY KEY,
 mechtype CHAR(10) NOT NULL
 CHECK (mechtype IN ('Primary', 'Assistant')),
 UNIQUE (jobid, mechtype));
```

because jobid is what identifies the entity that is represented by the table. In actual SQL implementations, the PRIMARY KEY declaration can affect data storage and access methods, so the choice could make a practical difference in performance.

PUZZLE

17 EMPLOYMENT AGENCY

Larry Wade posted a version of this problem on the MS-ACCESS Forum at the end of February 1996. He is running an employment service that has a database with tables for job orders, candidates, and their job skills. He is trying to do queries to match candidates to job orders based on their skills. The job orders take the form of a Boolean expression connecting skills. For example, find all candidates with manufacturing and inventory or accounting skills.

First, let's construct a table of the candidate's skills. You can assume that personal information about the candidate is in another table, but we will not bother with it for this problem.

```
CREATE TABLE CandidateSkills
(candidateid INTEGER NOT NULL,
 skill_code CHAR(15) NOT NULL,
 PRIMARY KEY (candidateid, skill_code));

INSERT INTO CandidateSkills
VALUES ((100, 'accounting'),
        (100, 'inventory'),
        (100, 'manufacturing'),
        (200, 'accounting'),
        (200, 'inventory'),
        (300, 'manufacturing'),
        (400, 'inventory'),
        (400, 'manufacturing'),
        (500, 'accounting'),
        (500, 'manufacturing'));
```

The obvious solution would be to create dynamic SQL queries in a front-end product for each job order, such as this:

```
SELECT candidateid, 'jobid #212' -- constant job id code
  FROM CandidateSkills AS C1, -- one correlation per skill
```

```
        CandidateSkills AS C2,
        CandidateSkills AS C3
 WHERE C1.candidateid = C2.candidateid
   AND C1.candidateid = C3.candidateid
   AND               -- job order expression created here
   (C1.skill_code = 'manufacturing'
    AND C2.skill_code = 'inventory'
     OR C3.skill_code = 'accounting')
```

A good PowerBuilder or Delphi programmer can come up with a screen form to do this in less than a week. You then save the query as a VIEW with the same name as the jobid code. Neat and quick! The trouble is that this solution will give you a huge collection of very slow queries.

Got a better idea? Oh, I forgot to mention that the number of job titles you have to handle is over 250,000. The agency is using the DOT (Dictionary of Occupational Titles), an encoding scheme used by the U.S. government for statistical purposes.

Answer #1

If we were not worrying about so many titles, the problem would be much easier. You could use an integer as a bit string and set the positions in the string to 1 or 0 for each occupation. For example:

'accounting' = 1
'inventory' = 2
'manufacturing' = 4
 etc.

Thus, ('inventory' AND 'manufacturing') can be represented by (2 + 4) = 6. Unfortunately, with a quarter of a million titles, this approach will not work.

The first problem is that you have to worry about parsing the search criteria. Does "manufacturing and inventory or accounting" mean "(manufacturing AND inventory) OR accounting" or does it mean "manufacturing AND (inventory OR accounting)" when you search? Let's assume that ANDs have higher precedence.

Answer #2

Another solution is to put every query into a disjunctive canonical form; what that means in English is that the search conditions are written as a string of AND-ed conditions joined together at the highest level by ORs.

Let's build another table of job orders that we want to fill:

```
CREATE TABLE JobOrders
(jobid INTEGER NOT NULL,
 skill_group INTEGER NOT NULL,
 skill_code CHAR(15) NOT NULL,
 PRIMARY KEY (jobid, skill_group, skill_code));
```

The skill_group code says that all these skills are required—they are the AND-ed terms in the canonical form. We can then assume that each skill_group in a job order is OR-ed with the others for that jobid. Create the table for the job orders. Now insert the following orders in their canonical form:

```
Job 1 = ('inventory' AND 'manufacturing') OR 'accounting'
Job 2 = ('inventory' AND 'manufacturing')
             OR ('accounting' AND 'manufacturing')
Job 3 = 'manufacturing'
Job 4 = ('inventory' AND 'manufacturing' AND 'accounting')
```

This translates into

```
INSERT INTO JobOrders
VALUES ((1, 1, 'inventory'),
        (1, 1, 'manufacturing'),
        (1, 2, 'accounting'),
        (2, 1, 'inventory'),
        (2, 1, 'manufacturing'),
        (2, 2, 'accounting'),
```

```
        (2, 2, 'manufacturing'),
        (3, 1, 'manufacturing'),
        (4, 1, 'inventory'),
        (4, 1, 'manufacturing'),
        (4, 1, 'accounting'));
```

The query is a form of relational division, based on using the skill_code and skill_group combinations as the dividend and the candidate's skills as the divisor. Since the skill_groups within a jobid are OR-ed together, if any one of them matches, we have a hit.

```
SELECT DISTINCT J1.jobid, C1.candidateid
   FROM JobOrders AS J1 INNER JOIN CandidateSkills AS C1
            ON J1.skill_code = C1.skill_code
  GROUP BY candidateid, skill_group, jobid
HAVING COUNT(*) >= (SELECT COUNT(*)
                      FROM JobOrders AS J2
                     WHERE J1.skill_group = J2.skill_group
                       AND J1.jobid = J2.jobid);
```

The sample data should produce the following results:

jobid	candidateid
1	100
1	200
1	400
1	500
2	100
2	400
2	500
3	100
3	300
3	400
3	500
4	100

As job orders and candidates are changed, the query stays the same. You can put this query into a VIEW, then use it to find the jobs for which we have no candidates, candidates for which we have no jobs, and so on.

Answer #3

Another answer came from Richard Romley, at Smith Barney. He then came up with an answer that does not involve a correlated subquery in SQL-92, thus:

```
SELECT J1.jobid, C1.candidateid
  FROM (SELECT jobid, skillgrp, COUNT(*)
          FROM JobSkillRequirements
        GROUP BY jobid, skillgrp)
        AS J1(jobid, skillgrp, grpct)
    CROSS JOIN
    (SELECT R1.jobid, R1.skillgrp, S1.candidateid, COUNT(*)
       FROM JobSkillRequirements AS R1, CandidateSkills AS S1
      WHERE R1.skillid = S1.skillid
      GROUP BY R1.jobid, R1.skillgrp, S1.candidateid)
      AS C1(jobid, skillgrp, candidateid, cct)
 WHERE J1.jobid = C1.jobid
   AND J1.skillgrp = C1.skillgrp
   AND J1.grpct = C1.cct
 GROUP BY J1.jobid, C1.candidateid;
```

Most current SQL implementations do not have the ability to do the subquery table expressions in the FROM, so just replace them with two VIEWs for C1 and J1.

I am also not sure how well the three GROUP BY statements will work compared to the correlated subquery. The grouped tables will not be able to use any indexing on the original tables, so this approach could be slower.

PUZZLE

18 JUNK MAIL

You are given a table with the addresses of consumers to whom we wish to send junk mail. The table has a `fam` (family) column that links Consumers with the same street address. We need this because our rules are that we mail only one offer to a household. The field contains the `PRIMARY KEY` value of the Consumers record of the first person who has this address, thus:

Consumers

name	address	id	fam
'Bob'	'A'	1	NULL
'Joe'	'B'	3	NULL
'Mark'	'C'	5	NULL
'Mary'	'A'	2	1
'Vickie'	'B'	4	3
'Wayne'	'D'	6	NULL

We need to delete those rows where `fam` is `NULL` but there are other family members on the mailing list. In the above example, I need to delete Bob and Joe, but not Mark and Wayne.

Answer #1

A first attempt might try to do too much work, but translating the English specification directly into SQL:

```
DELETE FROM Consumers
  WHERE fam IS NULL    -- this guy has a NULL family value
    AND EXISTS   -- ..and there is someone who is
        (SELECT *
           FROM Consumers AS C1
          WHERE C1.id <> id       -- a different person
            AND C1.address = address -- at the same address
            AND C1.fam IS NOT NULL); -- who has a family value
```

Answer #2

But if you think about it, you'll see that the COUNT(*) for the household has to be greater than 1.

```
DELETE FROM Consumers
 WHERE fam IS NULL    -- this guy has a NULL family value
   AND (SELECT COUNT(*)
          FROM Consumers AS C1
          WHERE C1.address = address) > 1;
```

The trick is that the COUNT(*) aggregate will include NULLs in its tally.

19 TOP SALESPERSONS

This problem came up in March 1995 at Database World, when someone came back from the IBM pavilion to talk to me. IBM had a DB2 expert with a whiteboard set up to answer questions and this one had stumped her. The problem starts with a table of salespersons and the amounts of their sales, which looks like this:

```
CREATE TABLE SalesData
(district INTEGER NOT NULL,
 salesperson CHAR(10) NOT NULL,
 salesid INTEGER NOT NULL,
 amount DECIMAL(5,2) NOT NULL);
```

The boss just came in and asked for a report that will tell him about the three biggest sales and salespersons in each district. Let's use this data:

SalesData

district	salesperson	salesid	amount
1	'Curly'	5	3.00
1	'Harpo'	11	4.00
1	'Larry'	1	50.00
1	'Larry'	2	50.00
1	'Larry'	3	50.00
1	'Moe'	4	5.00
2	'Dick'	8	5.00
2	'Fred'	7	5.00
2	'Harry'	6	5.00
2	'Tom'	7	5.00
3	'Irving'	10	5.00
3	'Melvin'	9	7.00

	district	salesperson	salesid	amount
(cont.)	4	'Jenny'	15	20.00
	4	'Jessie'	16	10.00
	4	'Mary'	12	50.00
	4	'Oprah'	14	30.00
	4	'Sally'	13	40.00

Answer

Unfortunately, there are some problems in the specification we got. Do we want the three largest sales (regardless of who made them) or the top three salespersons? There is a difference—look at district 1, where 'Larry' made all three of the largest sales, but the three best salespersons were 'Larry', 'Moe', and 'Harpo'.

What if more than three people sold exactly the same amount, as in district 2? If a district has fewer than three salespersons working in it, as in district 3, do we drop it from the report or not? Let us make the decision that the boss meant the three largest sales in each district, without regard to who the salespersons were. That query can be

```
SELECT *
  FROM SalesData AS S0
 WHERE amount IN (SELECT amount
                    FROM SalesData AS S1
                   WHERE S0.district = S1.district
                     AND S0.amount <= S1.amount
                  HAVING COUNT(*) <= 3)
 ORDER BY district, salesperson, salesid, amount;
```

In SQL-92, a HAVING clause by itself treats the whole table as a single group. If your SQL doesn't like this, replace the "amount IN (SELECT amount ..." with "amount >= (SELECT MIN(amount) ..." in the SELECT clause. If you do that, however, the HAVING clause will drop the districts with only one sales amount—district 2 in this case—giving these results:

Results

district	salesperson	salesid	amount
1	'Larry'	1	50.00
1	'Larry'	2	50.00
1	'Larry'	3	50.00
3	'Irving'	10	5.00
3	'Melvin'	9	7.00
4	'Mary'	12	50.00
4	'Oprah'	14	30.00
4	'Sally'	13	40.00

Now what if we wanted the top three salespersons in their districts, without regard to how many persons were assigned to each district? We could modify the query like this:

```
SELECT DISTINCT district, salesperson
  FROM SalesData AS S0
 WHERE amount <= (SELECT MAX(S1.amount)
                    FROM SalesData AS S1
                   WHERE S0.district = S1.district
                     AND S0.amount <= S1.amount
                  HAVING COUNT(DISTINCT amount) <= 3);
```

And get these results. Please notice that you are getting the three largest sales.

Answer

district	salesperson
1	'Harpo'
1	'Moe'
1	'Larry'
2	'Dick'
2	'Fred'

(cont.)

district	salesperson
2	'Harry'
2	'Tom'
3	'Irving'
3	'Melvin'
4	'Oprah'
4	'Sally'
4	'Mary'

Notice that the ties in district 2 gave us four people tied for the top three sales positions. Likewise, the lack of competition in district 3 gave us two salespersons in the top three.

PUZZLE
20 TEST RESULTS

A problem was posted on the CompuServe Sybase Forum in May 1995 by a Mr. Shankar. It had to do with a table of test results. This table tracks the progress of the testing by providing a completion date for each step in the test. The steps are not always done in order and each test can have several steps.

```
CREATE TABLE TestResults
(orderno INTEGER NOT NULL,
 step INTEGER NOT NULL,
 compdate DATE,
 PRIMARY KEY (orderno, step));
```

The problem was to write a quick query to find those tests that have not been completed yet.

Answer #1

I came up with the "obvious" answer:

```
SELECT orderno
  FROM TestResults AS T1
 WHERE NOT EXISTS (SELECT *
                     FROM TestResults AS T2
                    WHERE T1.orderno = T2.orderno
                      AND T2.compdate IS NULL);
```

Can you think of a different way to do it?

Answer #2

Roy Harvey had a better and simpler solution, based on a completely different approach:

```
SELECT orderno
  FROM TestResults
 GROUP BY orderno
HAVING COUNT(*) = COUNT(compdate);
```

This works because COUNT(*) will tally the NULLs in the compdate columns (actually, it's counting whole rows), while COUNT(compdate) will drop the NULLs before doing the tally. This is a good trick, which can be used when you need to compare one set to another.

PUZZLE

21 AIRPLANES AND PILOTS

We have a table of pilots and the planes they can fly and a table of planes in the hangar. We want the names of the pilots who can fly every plane in the hangar.

Answer #1

The classic answer is to pull out a copy of almost any textbook and look up relational division. Chris Date's fifth edition is a classic and gives a template that you can copy for this problem. We're dividing the pilot's skill table (dividend) by the hangar (divisor) to get a list of pilot names (quotient).

Can you find another way, which uses a trick we have already seen?

Answer #2

Look at the puzzle that came just before this problem. Roy Harvey's trick that we used in the Test Results Puzzle can be applied here. It's important to reuse tricks when you can.

Imagine that each pilot gets a set of stickers that he pastes to each plane in the hangar he can fly. If the number of planes in the hangar is the same as the number of stickers he used, he can fly all the planes in the hangar. That becomes the query:

```
SELECT Pilot
  FROM PilotSkills AS PS1, Hangar AS H1
 WHERE PS1.plane = H1.plane
 GROUP BY PS1.pilot
HAVING COUNT(PS1.plane) = (SELECT COUNT(*) FROM Hangar);
```

The WHERE clause restricts the PilotSkills plane list to those that are in the hangar before each pilot is grouped and tallied. If pilots were limited to only a subset of the hangar planes, you could drop the WHERE clause and use two COUNT (DISTINCT x) expressions instead of two COUNT(x) expressions.

PUZZLE

22 LANDLORD

Karen Gallaghar tried to use the following SQL (translated from the MS-ACCESS original) to do a report on who has paid their rent in an apartment complex:

```
SELECT *
  FROM Units AS U1
       LEFT OUTER JOIN
       (Tenants AS T1
        LEFT OUTER JOIN
        RentPaid AS RP1
         ON T1.tenantkey = RP1.tenantkey)
        ON U1.unitkey = T1.unitkey
 WHERE U1.complexkey = 32
   AND U1.unitkey = RP1.unitkey
   AND T1.movedout IS NULL
   AND ((RP1.datepaid >= :mydate
        AND RP1.datepaid < :mydate)
    OR RP1.datepaid IS NULL)
 ORDER BY U1.unitnumber, RP1.datepaid;
```

What she wanted was a report with either `RentPaid` records within the date range or blank `RentPaid` records for each unit/tenant combination. What happened was that she did not get blank records where there were no `RentPaid` records unless she dropped the `RentPaid` conditions. Can you see the problem and rewrite the query?

 Answer

The trick is to think about what is persistent and what is transient in a problem with `OUTER JOINs`. The unit-and-tenant pairs are the place to start: the unit stays, but the tenants come and go, so you need to preserve the unit side of the `LEFT OUTER JOIN`. Once you have the unit-and-tenant pairs, ask the same question and conclude that rent payments may come and go, even when you have a tenant in a unit.

```
SELECT *
 FROM (Units AS U1
       LEFT OUTER JOIN Tenants AS T1
       ON U1.unitkey = T1.unitkey
          AND T1.movedout IS NULL
          AND U1.complexkey = 32)
       LEFT OUTER JOIN RentPaid AS RP1
       ON (T1.tenantkey = RP1.tenantkey
          AND U1.unitkey = RP1.unitkey)
   WHERE ((RP1.datepaid >= :mydate
          AND RP1.datepaid < :mydate)
     OR RP1.datepaid IS NULL)
 ORDER BY U1.unitnumber, RP1.datepaid;
```

The predicate (`T1.tenantkey = RP1.tenantkey AND U1.unitkey = RP1.unitkey`) is saying that a particular tenant has paid rent for a particular unit. This is to cover the situations where the same party rents more than one unit in the complex. You may assume that referential constraints prevent you from collecting rent from someone who does not have a unit.

PUZZLE
23 MAGAZINE

This one was posted on the Sybase Forum of CompuServe by Keith McGregor in November 1994. One of his end users came to him with the following query: After nearly three days of trial and error, he still doesn't have a clue as to how to tell her to do it. He could have done this in about 30 minutes using Cobol and flat files, but didn't see any way in SQL.

You are given the following tables for a magazine distribution database:

```
CREATE TABLE Titles
(product_id INTEGER NOT NULL PRIMARY KEY,
 title INTEGER NOT NULL,
 issue INTEGER NOT NULL,
 issue_year INTEGER NOT NULL);


CREATE TABLE Sales
(product_id INTEGER NOT NULL,
 standno INTEGER NOT NULL,
 net_sold_qty INTEGER NOT NULL,
 PRIMARY KEY (product_id, customer));


CREATE TABLE Newsstands
(standno INTEGER NOT NULL PRIMARY KEY
 stand_name CHAR (20) NOT NULL);
```

He needed to select the newsstand(s) where:

1. The average net_sold_qty is greater than 2 for *both* title 02667 and title 48632 (if the average is 2 or less for either one, do not select the customer at all).

    or

2. The average net_sold_qty is greater than 5 for title 01107 (if this is true, select the customer regardless of the result of condition 1).

Answer #1

Let's create a VIEW of the three tables joined together that will give us the basic information we're after. Maybe this VIEW can be used for other reports later.

```
CREATE VIEW Magazine(stand_name, title, net_sold_qty)
AS SELECT Sales.stand_name, Titles.title, net_sold_qty
  FROM Titles, Sales, Newsstands
 WHERE Sales.standno = Newsstands.standno
   AND Titles.product_id = Sales.product_id;
```

Then we write the Query from Hell:

```
SELECT stand_name
 FROM Magazines AS M0
GROUP BY stand_name
 HAVING  -- the two accept conditions
   ((SELECT AVG(net_sold_qty)
      FROM Magazines AS M1
     WHERE M1.standno = M0.standno
       AND title = '01107') > 5)
   OR ((SELECT AVG(net_sold_qty)
          FROM Magazines AS M2
         WHERE M2.standno = M0.standno
           AND title IN ('02667', '48632')) > 2)
 AND NOT -- the two reject conditions
     ((SELECT AVG(net_sold_qty)
        FROM Magazines AS M3
       WHERE M3.standno = M0.standno
         AND title IN = '02667') < 2
       OR
       (SELECT AVG(net_sold_qty)
          FROM Magazines AS M4
```

```
      WHERE M4.standno = M0.standno
        AND title = '48632') < 2);
```

For bonus points, can you simplify or improve this expression?

HINT: *DeMorgan's law might be useful and it would help to have a decision table.*

Answer #2

In April 1995, Carl C. Federl, an independent consultant in Clarendon Hills, Illinois, proposed that the solution provided for this puzzle could be greatly simplified by using two techniques: First create a VIEW of the average sales and include an EXISTS() for the condition of two titles that both must exceed a threshold.

```
CREATE VIEW Magazines (standno, title, avg_qty_sold)
AS SELECT Sales.standno, Titles.title, AVG(Sales.net_sold_qty)
    FROM Titles, Newsstands, Sales
   WHERE Titles.product_id = Sales.product_id
     AND Newsstands.standno = Sales.standno
     AND Titles.title IN (01107, 02667, 48632)
   GROUP BY Sales.standno, Titles.title;
```

Now the query is greatly reduced:

```
SELECT DISTINCT Newsstands.stand_name
  FROM Magazines AS M0, Newsstands AS N0
 WHERE N0.standno = M0.standno
   AND ((M0.title = 1107 AND M0.avg_qty_sold > 5)
      OR (M0.title = 2667 AND M0.avg_qty_sold > 2
        AND EXISTS (SELECT *
                     FROM Magazines AS Other
                    WHERE Other.title = 48632
                      AND Other.standno = M0.standno
                      AND Other.avg_qty_sold > 2)));
```

In older versions of Sybase SQL and other databases, a VIEW with an aggregate that is joined will not produce the desired results. Instead of a VIEW, a temporary table must be used.

PUZZLE
24 ONE IN TEN

Alan Flancman ran into a problem with some legacy system data that had been moved over to an SQL database. The table looked like this:

```
CREATE TABLE MyTable
(keycol INTEGER NOT NULL,
 f1 INTEGER NOT NULL,
 f2 INTEGER NOT NULL,
 ...
 f10 INTEGER NOT NULL,
 );
```

The columns f1 thru f10 were an attempt to flatten out an array into a table. What he wanted was an elegant way to test against the f1 thru f10 columns to find each row that had exactly one nonzero value in its columns.

How many different approaches can you find? We're looking for variety and not for performance.

Answer #1

You could use the SIGN() function in Sybase and other SQL products. This function returns –1, 0, or +1 if the argument is negative, zero, or positive, respectively. Assuming that your numbers are zero or greater, you simply write

```
SELECT *
  FROM MyTable
 WHERE SIGN(f1) + SIGN(f2) + ... + SIGN(f10) = 1;
```

to find a single nonzero value. If you can have negative values, make the functions SIGN(ABS(fn)).

The SIGN() function can be written with the CASE expression in SQL-92 as

```
CASE WHEN x > 0 THEN 1
     WHEN x = 0 THEN 0
     ELSE -1 END
```

Answer #2

Since the fields are really an attempt to fake an array, you should normalize this table into 1NF, like this:

```
CREATE TABLE Foobar
(keycol INTEGER NOT NULL,
 i INTEGER NOT NULL CHECK (i BETWEEN 1 AND 10),
 f INTEGER NOT NULL,
 PRIMARY KEY (keycol, i));
```

The extra column i is really the subscript for the array. You now view the problem as finding an entity that has exactly nine zero-valued f's, instead of finding an entity that has exactly one nonzero-valued f. That is suddenly easy:

```
SELECT keycol
  FROM Foobar
 WHERE f = 0
 GROUP BY keycol
HAVING COUNT(*) = 9;
```

You can create a VIEW that has the structure of Foobar, but things are going to run pretty slowly unless you have a good optimizer:

```
CREATE VIEW Foobar (keycol, f)
AS SELECT keycol, f1 FROM MyTable
   UNION
   SELECT keycol, f2 FROM MyTable
   UNION
   ...
   UNION
   SELECT keycol, f10 FROM MyTable;
```

Answer #3

This depends on a feature of SQL-92 that is not generally available yet. First the code, then the explanation:

```
SELECT *
  FROM MyTable
 WHERE (f1, f2, ... , f10) IN
     ((f1, 0, 0, 0, 0, 0, 0, 0, 0, 0),
      (0, f2, 0, 0, 0, 0, 0, 0, 0, 0),
       ....
      (0, 0, 0, 0, 0, 0, 0, 0, 0, f10));,
```

In SQL-92, you can use row constructors in comparison predicates. The IN( ) predicate expands into a sequence of OR-ed equality predicates. The row-wise version of equality is then done on a position-by-position basis, where all corresponding values must be equal.

Answer #4

If one and only one column is nonzero, there is one set of nine columns that are all zeroes.

```
SELECT *
  FROM MyTable
 WHERE (f2 + f3 + .. f10) = 0 -- pull out f1
    OR (f1 + f3 + .. f10) = 0 -- pull out f2
     ...
    OR (f1 + f2 + .. f9) = 0; -- pull out f10
```

PUZZLE
25 MILESTONE

This puzzle, in a slightly different form, came from Brian Young. His system tracks a series of dates (milestones) for each particular type of service (tos) that the company sells. These dates constitute the schedule for the delivery of the service and vary with the type of service they are delivering. Their management would like to see a schedule for each shop horizontally, which I must admit is a reasonable request. They also want to be able to specify the task code (tos) to display.

Brian ran across a clever solution to this problem by Steve Roti in an SQL server book, but it relies on the SUM( ) function and a multiplication by 1 to yield the correct result. (That Roti guy is very clever!) Unfortunately, this technique doesn't work with dates. So here is the table structure:

```
CREATE TABLE Schedule
(shop CHAR (3) NOT NULL,
 order CHAR (10) NOT NULL,
 schseq SMALLINT NOT NULL CHECK (schseq IN (1,2,3),
 tos CHAR (2) NOT NULL,
 schactdate DATE);
```

where schseq is encoded as

  (1 = 'processed')
  (2 = 'completed')
  (3 = 'confirmed')

The data normally appears like this:

Schedule

shop	order	schseq	tos	schactdate
002	4155526710	1	01	'1994-07-16'
002	4155526710	2	01	'1994-07-30'

	shop	order	schseq	tos	schactdate
(cont.)	002	4155526710	3	01	'1994-10-01'
	002	4155526711	1	01	'1994-07-16'
	002	4155526711	2	01	'1994-07-30'
	002	4155526711	3	01	NULL

This is the way they would like it to appear, assuming they want to look at (tos = 01):

order	processed	completed	confirmed
4155526710	'1994-07-16'	'1994-07-16'	'1994-10-01'
4155526711	'1994-07-16'	'1994-07-16'	NULL

Answer #1

In SQL-92, this is easy and very fast with subquery expressions:

```
SELECT order,
    (SELECT schactdate
      FROM Schedule AS S1
    WHERE S1.schseq = 1
      AND S1.order = S0.order) AS processed,
    (SELECT schactdate
      FROM Schedule AS S2
    WHERE S2.schseq = 2
      AND S2.order = S0.order) AS completed,
    (SELECT schactdate
      FROM Schedule AS S3
    WHERE S3.schseq = 3
      AND S3.order = S0.order) AS confirmed
  FROM Schedule AS S0
  WHERE tos = :myorder; -- set task code
```

The trouble with the new tricks is that they may not be optimized in your SQL.

Answer #2

Another trick involves using self-joins, which will work in SQL-89 as well as SQL-92.

```
SELECT S0.order.schactdate, S0.schactdate,
       S1.schactdate, S2.schactdate, S3.schactdate
 FROM Schedule AS S0, Schedule AS S1,
      Schedule AS S2, Schedule AS S3
 WHERE S0.tos = :mytos -- set task code
   AND S0.order = :myorder -- set order
   AND S1.order = S0.order AND S1.schseq = 1
   AND S2.order = S0.order AND S2.schseq = 2
   AND S3.order = S0.order AND S3.schseq = 3;
```

The problem is that for some SQL products, the self-joins are very expensive. This is probably the fastest answer on most current SQL products. Can you think of another way?

Answer #3

You could try using UNIONs and a work table to flatten out the original table. This is not usually a very good performer, but if the original table is very large, it can sometimes beat the self-join used in Answer #2.

```
INSERT INTO Work (order, processed, completed, confirmed)
SELECT order, NULL, NULL, NULL
 FROM Schedule AS S0
 WHERE tos = :myorder -- set task code
UNION
SELECT order, schactdate, NULL, NULL
  FROM Schedule AS S1
  WHERE S1.schseq = 1
   AND S1.order = :myorder
   AND tos = :mytos -- set task code
```

```
UNION
 SELECT order, NULL, schactdate, NULL
  FROM Schedule AS S2
  WHERE S2.schseq = 2
   AND S2.order = :myorder
   AND tos = :mytos -- set task code
UNION
 SELECT order, NULL, NULL, schactdate
  FROM Schedule AS S3
  WHERE S3.schseq = 3
   AND S3.order = :myorder
   AND tos = :mytos -- set task code
```

This simple UNION may have to be broken down into four INSERTs.
The final query is simply

```
SELECT order, MAX(processed), MAX(completed), MAX(confirmed)
 FROM Work
GROUP BY order;
```

The MAX() function picks the highest non-NULL value in
the group, which also happens to be the only non-NULL value in
the group.

PUZZLE
26 DATAFLOW DIAGRAMS

Tom Bragg posted a version of this problem on the CASE Forum on CompuServe. You have a table of dataflow diagrams (DFDs), which has the name of the diagram, the names of the bubbles in each diagram, and the labels on the flow lines. It looks like this:

```
CREATE TABLE DFD
(diagram CHAR(10) NOT NULL,
 bubble CHAR(10) NOT NULL,
 flow CHAR(10) NOT NULL,
 PRIMARY KEY (diagram, bubble, flow));
```

To explain the problem, let's use this table:

DFD

diagram	bubble	flow
Proc1	input	guesses
Proc1	input	opinions
Proc1	crunch	facts
Proc1	crunch	guesses
Proc1	crunch	opinions
Proc1	output	facts
Proc1	output	guesses
Proc2	reckon	guesses
Proc2	reckon	opinions
. . .		

What we want to find is what flows do *not* go into each bubble within the diagrams. This will be part of a diagram validation routine that will search for missing dataflows. To make this easier, assume that all bubbles should have all flows. This would mean that (Proc1, input) is missing the 'facts' flow and that (Proc1, output) is missing the 'opinions' flow.

Answer #1

We could use this SQL-92 query:

```
SELECT F1.diagram, F1.bubble, F2.flow
 FROM (SELECT F1.diagram, F1.bubble FROM DFD AS F1
       CROSS JOIN
       SELECT DISTINCT F2.flow FROM DFD AS F2)
       EXCEPT
       SELECT F3.diagram, F3.bubble, F3.flow FROM DFD AS F3
 ORDER BY F1.diagram, F1.bubble, F2.flow;
```

Basically, it makes all possible combinations of diagrams and flows, then removes the ones we already have. The bad news is that you will probably have to do this with VIEWs in most current SQL products.

Answer #2

Another SQL-92 query would be

```
SELECT F1.diagram, F1.bubble, F2.flow
 FROM (SELECT F1.diagram, F1.bubble FROM DFD AS F1)
       CROSS JOIN
       (SELECT DISTINCT F2.flow
          FROM DFD AS F2
        WHERE flow NOT IN (SELECT F3.flow
                             FROM DFD AS F3
                            WHERE F3.diagram = F1.diagram
                              AND F3.bubble = F1.bubble))
 ORDER BY F1.diagram, F1.bubble, F2.flow;
```

Answer #3

Or to answer the puzzle in SQL-89, you will need to use VIEWs:

```
-- build a set of all the flows
CREATE VIEW AllDFDFlows (flow)
AS SELECT DISTINCT flow FROM DFD;
```

```
-- attach all the flows to each row of the original table
CREATE VIEW NewDFD (diagram, bubble, flow, missingflow)
SELECT DISTINCT F1.diagram, F1.bubble, F1.flow, F2.flow
 FROM DFD AS F1, AllDFDFlows AS F2
WHERE F1.flow <> F2.flow;

-- Show me the (diagram, bubble) pairs and missing flow
-- where the missing flow was not somewhere in the flow column
-- of the pair.
SELECT DISTINCT diagram, bubble, missingflow
 FROM NewDFD AS ND1
WHERE NOT EXISTS (SELECT *
                   FROM NewDFD AS ND2
                  WHERE ND1.diagram = ND2.diagram
                    AND ND1.bubble = ND2.bubble
                    AND ND1.flow = ND2.missingflow)
ORDER BY diagram, bubble, missingflow;
```

I probably overdid the DISTINCTs, but you can experiment with it for execution speed. This should still run faster than moving all the rows across the network.

27 FINDING EQUAL SETS

Set theory has two symbols for subsets. One is a "horseshoe" on its side (⊂), which means "is contained within," as in "set A is contained within set B," and is sometimes called a proper subset. The other is the same symbol with a horizontal bar under it (⊆), which means "is contained within or equal to," which is sometimes just called a subset or containment operator.

Standard SQL has never had an operator to compare tables against each other. Several college textbooks on relational databases mention a CONTAINS predicate that does not exist in standard SQL-89 and was not proposed for SQL-92. Two such offenders are *An Introduction to Data Base Systems,* by Bipin C. Desai (West Publishing, 1990, ISBN 0-314-66771-7) and *Fundamentals of Database Systems,* by Elmasri and Navthe (Benjamin Cummings, 1989, ISBN 0-8053-0145-3). This predicate did exist in the original System R, IBM's first experimental SQL system, but it was dropped from later SQL implementations because of the expense of running it. The IN() predicate is a test for membership, not for subsets. For those of you who remember your high school set theory, membership is shown by a stylized epsilon (∈) with the containing set on the right side of it. Membership is for one element; a subset is itself a set, not just an element.

Chris Date's puzzle in the December issue of *Database Programming & Design* magazine ("A Matter of Integrity, Part II" According to Date, December 1993) was to use a suppliers-and-parts table to find pairs of suppliers that provide *exactly* the same parts. This is the same thing as finding two equal sets. Given this table:

```
CREATE TABLE SupParts
(sno CHAR(2) NOT NULL,
 pno CHAR(2) NOT NULL,
 PRIMARY KEY (sno, pno));
```

How many ways can you find to do this problem?

Answer #1

One approach would be to do a FULL OUTER JOIN on each pair of suppliers. Any parts that are not common to both would show up, but would have generated NULLs in one of the columns derived from the supplier who was not in the INNER JOIN portion. This tells you which pairs are not matched, not who is. The final step is to remove these nonmatching pairs from all possible pairs.

```
SELECT SP1.sno, SP2.sno
  FROM SupParts AS SP1
       INNER JOIN
       SupParts AS SP2
EXCEPT
(SELECT DISTINCT SP1.sno, SP2.sno
  FROM SupParts AS SP1
       FULL OUTER JOIN
       SupParts AS SP2
         ON SP1.pno = SP2.pno
            AND SP1.sno < SP2.sno)
 WHERE SP1.sno IS NULL
    OR SP2.sno IS NULL;
```

This is probably going to run very slowly.

Answer #2

The usual way of proving that two sets are equal to each other is to show that set A contains set B and set B contains set A. What you would usually do in standard SQL would be to show that there exists no element in set A that is not in set B and therefore A is a subset of B: $(A \subset B \land B \subset A) \rightarrow (A = B)$. So the first attempt is usually something like this:

```
SELECT DISTINCT SP1.sno, SP2.sno
  FROM SupParts AS SP1, SupParts AS SP2
 WHERE SP1.sno < SP2.sno
   AND SP1.pno IN (SELECT SP22.pno
```

```
                FROM SupParts AS SP22
               WHERE SP22.sno = SP2.sno)
       AND SP2.pno IN (SELECT SP11.pno
                FROM SupParts AS SP11
               WHERE SP11.sno = SP1.sno);
```

Oops, this does not work, because if two suppliers have one item in common, they will be returned.

Answer #3

You can use the ALL predicate to imply the traditional test mentioned in Answer #2.

```
SELECT SP1.sno, SP2.sno
  FROM SupParts AS SP1. SupParts AS SP2
 WHERE SP1.sno < SP2.sno
   AND NOT EXISTS (SELECT *
                    FROM SupParts AS SP3
                   WHERE SP1.sno = SP3.sno
                     AND SP1.pno
                         NOT IN (SELECT pno
                                   FROM SupParts AS SP4
                                  WHERE SP2.sno = SP4.sno))
   AND NOT EXISTS (SELECT *
                    FROM SupParts AS SP5
                   WHERE SP2.sno = SP5.sno
                     AND SP2.pno
                         NOT IN (SELECT pno
                                   FROM SupParts AS SP4
                                  WHERE SP1.sno = SP4.sno));
```

Answer #4

The traditional way to do set equality: First I join one supplier to another on their common parts, eliminating the situation where supplier 1 is the same as supplier 2, so that I have the intersection of the two sets. If the intersection has the same number of pairs as each of the two sets has elements, the two sets are equal.

```
SELECT SP1.sno, SP2.sno
  FROM (SELECT sno, pno FROM SupParts) AS SP1
       INNER JOIN
       (SELECT sno, pno FROM SupParts AS SP2
       ON SP1.pno = SP2.pno
          AND SP1.sno < SP2.sno)
 GROUP BY SP1.sno, SP2.sno
HAVING (SELECT COUNT(*)
          FROM SupParts AS SP3
         WHERE SP3.sno = SP1.sno)
     = (SELECT COUNT(*)
          FROM SupParts AS SP4
         WHERE SP4.sno = SP2.sno);
```

If there is an index on the supplier number in the SupParts table, it can provide the counts directly and also help with the JOIN operation.

CHAPTER

4

Computing Things

SQL IS NOT a computational language. The ANSI/ISO standard SQL-92 language defines only four-function arithmetic, making it weaker than a good calculator wristwatch. However, most vendors have added function library routines from other compilers into their SQL products, so you can usually get computational power if you need it. The current ANSI/ISO SQL3 proposals have more library routines defined in the language. Vendors can now borrow the function choices and syntax for their own products even before the SQL3 document is approved as a standard.

The functions you'll have to write in SQL will be either aggregate functions that SQL does not support or scalar functions.

It's easy to do the standard scalar functions, such as sin(), cos(), and so forth, by making a table and doing table lookup. A slightly fancier trick is to write a query with an interpolation calculation in it or in a VIEW.

The hard scalar functions usually involve picking values from multiple tables and calculating a result from them.

PUZZLE

28 CALCULATE THE SINE FUNCTION

Let's assume that your SQL product does not have a sine function in its standard library. Can you write a query that will calculate the sine of a number in radians?

Answer #1

Just create a table with all the values you need:

```
CREATE TABLE Sine
(x REAL NOT NULL,
 sin REAL NOT NULL);

INSERT INTO Sine VALUES (0.00, 0.0000);
 ...
INSERT INTO Sine VALUES (0.75  0.6816);
INSERT INTO Sine VALUES (0.76  0.6889);
 ...
  etc.
```

You can fill in this table with the help of a spreadsheet. You can now use this table in the following scalar subquery to find sin(:myvalue):

```
(SELECT sin FROM Sine WHERE x = :myvalue)
```

Of course, the table can get pretty big for some functions, but for smaller functions with a limited range of argument values, this is not a bad approach. The sine just happens to be a horrible choice, since it is a continuous function defined over all real numbers.

Answer #2

Did you notice that if :myvalue in the first answer was not in the table, the subquery would be empty and hence return a NULL? This is not good.

If you get out an old calculus or trigonometry book, you'll find out how your ancestors used tables in the days before there were calculators. They had a mathematical technique called interpolation, which came in several flavors.

The easiest method is linear interpolation. Given two known values of a function, f(a) and f(b), you can approximate a third value of the function that lies between them. The formula is

f(a) + (x-a) * ((f(b) - f(a))/ (b-a))

For example, assume we want to find sin(0.754) and the table only has the values

```
INSERT INTO Sine VALUES (0.75  0.6816);
INSERT INTO Sine VALUES (0.76  0.6889);
```

We plug in the formula and get

0.6816 + (0.754 - 0.75) * ((0.6889 - 0.6816)/ (0.76 - 0.75)) = .68452

The trick is to put it in a query:

```
SELECT A.sin + (:myvalue - A.x)
       * ((B.sin - A.sin)/ (B.x - A.x))
  FROM Sine AS A, Sine AS B
 WHERE A.x = (SELECT MAX(x) FROM Sine WHERE x <= :myvalue)
   AND B.x = (SELECT MIN(x) FROM Sine WHERE x >= :myvalue);
```

There are other interpolation methods, but the basic idea is the same.

29 FIND THE MODE

I assume the reader knows that the only descriptive statistical function in SQL is the simple average, AVG(). While it is a common statistic, it is not the only one. Paul Dong posted a query that would find the most common values in a column in a table. This is called the *mode* in statistics. Let's suppose that the table is named "Payroll" and has the paycheck number and amount of each paycheck.

```
CREATE TABLE Payroll
(paycheck INTEGER NOT NULL PRIMARY KEY,
 salary DECIMAL(8,2) NOT NULL,
 ... );
```

What we want to see is the most common salary amount and its number of occurrences on the payroll. How would you write this query in SQL-89? In SQL-92?

Answer #1

SQL-89 lacks the orthogonality that SQL-92 has, so the best way is probably to build a VIEW first:

```
CREATE VIEW SalaryCounts
AS SELECT COUNT(*) AS paycheck_count
     FROM Payroll
    GROUP BY salary;
```

Then use the VIEW to find the most frequent salary amount:

```
SELECT salary, COUNT(*)
  FROM Payroll
 GROUP BY salary
HAVING COUNT(*) = (SELECT MAX(paycheck_count)
                   FROM SalaryCounts);
```

But this solution leaves a VIEW lying around the database schema. If you need it for something else, this is handy, but otherwise it is clutter. It would be better to do this in one statement without VIEWs.

Answer #2

The orthogonality of SQL-92 will allow you to fold the VIEW into a tabular subquery, thus:

```
SELECT salary, COUNT(*)
  FROM Payroll
 GROUP BY salary
HAVING COUNT(*) = (SELECT MAX(paycheck_count)
                     FROM (SELECT COUNT(*) AS paycheck_count
                             FROM Payroll
                            GROUP BY salary));
```

The innermost SELECT statement has to be expanded completely before it passes the grouped table to its immediate containing SELECT statement. That statement finds the MAX() and then passes that single number to the outermost SELECT. There is a very good chance that the grouped table will be destroyed in this process. If the optimizer were smart, it would have saved the first query to reuse in the final answer, but don't bet on it. Let's keep looking.

Answer #3

Here is another SQL-92 solution that will handle NULLs a bit differently than the last solution; can you tell me what the differences are?

```
SELECT PO.salary, COUNT(*)
  FROM Payroll
 GROUP BY salary
HAVING COUNT(*) >= ALL (SELECT COUNT(*)
                          FROM Payroll
                         GROUP BY salary);
```

The possible advantage of this answer is that since no MAX( ) function is used, there is a better chance that the grouped table will be preserved from one SELECT to be used by the other. Notice that the innermost SELECT is a projection of the outermost SELECT.

You should try all three solutions to see how your particular SQL implementation will perform with them.

30 AVERAGE SALES WAIT

Raymond Petersen asked me the following question: Given a Sales table with date-of-the-sale and customer columns, is there any way to calculate the average number of days between sales for each customer in a single SQL statement? Use a simple table in which you can assume that nobody makes more than one sale to the same person on the same day:

```
CREATE TABLE Sales
(customer CHAR(5) NOT NULL,
 salesdate DATE NOT NULL,
 PRIMARY KEY (customer, saledate));
```

Let's take a look at the date for the first week in June:

Sales

customer	saledate
'Fred'	'1994-06-01'
'Mary'	'1994-06-01'
'Bill'	'1994-06-01'
'Fred'	'1994-06-02'
'Bill'	'1994-06-02'
'Bill'	'1994-06-03'
'Bill'	'1994-06-04'
'Bill'	'1994-06-05'
'Bill'	'1994-06-06'
'Bill'	'1994-06-07'
'Fred'	'1994-06-07'
'Mary'	'1994-06-08'

The data shows that Fred waited one day, then waited five days, for an average of three days between his visits. Mary waited seven days, for an average of seven days. Bill is a regular customer every day.

Answer #1

The first impulse is to construct an elaborate VIEW that shows the number of days following each purchase for each customer. The first task in this approach is to get the sales into a table with the current saledate and the date of the last purchase:

```
CREATE VIEW Lastsales (customer, thissaledate, lastsaledate)
 AS SELECT S1.customer, S1.saledate,
     (SELECT MAX(saledate)
       FROM Sales AS S2
       WHERE S2.saledate < S1.saledate
         AND S2.customer = S1.customer)
    FROM Sales AS S1, Sales AS S2;
```

This is a greatest lower bound query—we want the highest date in the set of dates for this customer that comes before the current date.

Now we construct a VIEW with the gap in days between this sale and the customer's last purchase. You could combine the two views in one statement, but it would be unreadable and would probably not optimize any better.

```
CREATE VIEW SalesGap (customer, gap)
AS SELECT customer, DAYS(thissaledate, lastsaledate)
   FROM Lastsales;
```

The final answer is one query:

```
SELECT customer, AVG(gap)
 FROM SalesGap
GROUP BY customer;
```

You could combine the two views into the AVG( ) parameter, but it would be totally unreadable, might blow up, and would run like molasses.

Answer #2

I showed you Answer #1 because it demonstrates how you can be too smart for your own good. Because we only look for the average number of days a customer waits between purchases, there is no need to build an elaborate VIEW. Simply count the total number of days elapsed and then divide by the number of sales.

```
SELECT customer, (MAX(saledate) - MIN(saledate)) / (COUNT(*)-1)
  FROM Sales
 GROUP BY customer
HAVING COUNT(*) > 1;
```

The (COUNT(*)-1) works because there is always one less gap than there are orders if you do not consider the time gap between the date of the last order and today's date. The HAVING clause will remove from consideration customers who have made only one purchase. These one-shot customers can be included by changing MAX(saledate) to CURRENT_DATE in the SELECT statement. Incidentally, with either approach, you can have more than one sale per day per customer.

31 BUYING ALL THE PRODUCTS

Software AG introduced an intelligent SQL query-writing product called Esperant. Using the keyboard and an interactive pick list, the user constructs an English sentence, which the machine turns into a series of target SQL queries.

Yes, natural-language queries are an old idea, but most of them have involved some preprogramming of English phrases to make them work. The amount of work that Esperant can do by itself is what makes it worth looking at. It will generate relational divisions, create VIEWs, and build complex transactions without any preprogramming. Software AG's demo had a table of customers, orders, and order detail lines.

```
CREATE TABLE Customers
(customer_id INTEGER NOT NULL,
 balance DECIMAL (12,2) NOT NULL,
 ... );

CREATE TABLE Orders
(customer_id INTEGER NOT NULL,
 order_id INTEGER NOT NULL,
 ... );

CREATE TABLE Details
(order_id INTEGER NOT NULL,
 item_id INTEGER NOT NULL,
 ... );

CREATE TABLE Products
(item_id INTEGER NOT NULL,
 qty INTEGER NOT NULL,
```

Part of one sample problem was to find the average customer balance for all customers who had orders for all products and the average customer balance for all customers who did not have orders for all of the products. Esperant did an impressive job, but it generated a lot of VIEWs for portability. Using some of the new SQL-92 constructs or making better use of the old SQL-89 constructs, can you improve on this query?

Answer #1

The traditional answer is to use a deeply nested query. This query would translate into "Find the average for the set of customers for whom there is a product that is not in their orders" in English.

```
SELECT AVG(balance)
  FROM Customers AS C1
 WHERE EXISTS
       (SELECT *
          FROM Products AS P1
         WHERE P1.item
               NOT IN (SELECT D1.item
                         FROM Orders AS O1, Details AS D1
                        WHERE O1.customer_id = C1.customer_id
                          AND O1.customer_id = D1.customer_id));
```

To get the average balance of the customers, you could change EXISTS() to NOT EXISTS().

Answer #2

Gillian Robertson, of Worcestershire, England, found a neat trick that saves some of the nesting of correlated subqueries.

```
SELECT AVG(balance)
  FROM Customers AS C1
 WHERE (SELECT COUNT(DISTINCT prod) FROM Products)
       <> (SELECT COUNT(DISTINCT prod)
             FROM Orders, Details
            WHERE Orders.customer_id = C1.customer_id);
```

This will find the average balance of all customers who do not buy all products, by ensuring that the number of distinct items that show up in their order details is not the number of distinct items in the product list. Obviously, changing "<>" to "=" returns the customers who did order everything we sell.

PUZZLE

32 TAX CALCULATIONS

Richard Romley sent this problem via CompuServe. It's a simplified version of a problem related to tax calculations. I will define a tax area as being made up of multiple tax authorities. For example, a tax area might be a city, and the tax authorities for that city might be the city, the city's county, and the state. When you pay tax on a purchase in the city, the tax rate you pay is made up of the city tax, the county tax, and the state tax. Each of these taxing authorities changes its tax rate independently.

You have the following table:

```
CREATE TABLE TaxAreaAuthority
(taxauthority CHAR(10) NOT NULL,
 taxarea CHAR(10) NOT NULL,
 PRIMARY KEY (taxauthority, taxarea));
```

This is a hierarchy in which each tax area pays the multiple tax authorities to which it belongs:

TaxAreaAuthority

taxauthority	taxarea
'city1'	'city1'
'city2'	'city2'
'city3'	'city3'
'county1'	'city1'
'county1'	'city2'
'county2'	'city3'
'state1'	'city1'
'state1'	'city2'
'state1'	'city3'

This means that city1 and city2 are in county1 of state1, city3 is in county2 of state 1, and so forth. The other table you need is the tax rates, as follows:

```
CREATE TABLE TaxRates
(taxauthority CHAR(10) NOT NULL,
 dteffective DATE NOT NULL,
 authtaxrate DECIMAL (8,2) NOT NULL,
 PRIMARY KEY (taxauthority, dteffective));
```

Populate this table as follows:

TaxRates

taxauthority	dteffective	authtaxrate
'city1'	'1993-01-01'	1.0
'city1'	'1994-01-01'	1.5
'city2'	'1993-09-01'	1.5
'city2'	'1994-01-01'	2.0
'city2'	'1995-01-01'	2.5
'city3'	'1993-01-01'	1.7
'city3'	'1993-07-01'	1.9
'county1'	'1993-01-01'	2.3
'county1'	'1994-10-01'	2.5
'county1'	'1995-01-01'	2.7
'county2'	'1993-01-01'	2.4
'county2'	'1994-01-01'	2.7
'county2'	'1995-01-01'	2.8
'state1'	'1993-01-01'	0.5
'state1'	'1994-01-01'	0.8
'state1'	'1994-07-01'	0.9
'state1'	'1994-10-01'	1.1

This table is to be used for answering problems such as "What is the total tax rate for city2 on November 1, 1994?" for the tax collector. The answer for this particular question would be

```
City2 taxrate    = 2.0
County1 taxrate = 2.5
State1 taxrate    = 1.1
_____
TotalTaxRate    = 5.6
```

Can you write a single SQL-92 query to answer this question?

Answer

It is best to solve this problem in pieces. First, you want to find out who the taxing authorities for the city are, so you write a subquery:

```
(SELECT taxauthority
FROM TaxAreaAuthority AS A1
WHERE A1.taxarea = 'city2')
```

This will result in the set ('city2', 'county1', 'state1').

Next, you want to find out what the tax rates were on November 1, 1994, so you write another subquery:

```
(SELECT taxauthority, authtaxrate
   FROM TaxRates AS R1
  WHERE R1.dteffective = (SELECT MAX (R2.dteffective)
                            FROM TaxRates AS R2
                           WHERE R2.dteffective
                           <= '1994-11-01'))
```

Now combine the two subqueries, do a summation, and put your constants in the SELECT list to make the final answer readable. Actually, I would change these constants into parameters to generalize the routine, but, for now, let's stick to the original problem:

```
SELECT 'city2' AS city,  '1994-11-01' AS effective_date,
       SUM (authtaxrate) AS total_taxes
   FROM TaxRates AS R1
  WHERE R1.dteffective =
        (SELECT MAX (R2.dteffective)
           FROM TaxRates AS R2
          WHERE R2.dteffective <= '1994-11-01'
            AND R1.taxauthority = R2.taxauthority)
            AND R2.taxauthority IN (SELECT taxauthority
                                      FROM TaxAreaAuthority
                                      AS A1
                                     WHERE A1.taxarea
                                     - 'city2')
  GROUP BY city, effective_date;
```

But wait! You can do more consolidation and move the second AND predicate to a deeper level of nesting, like this:

```
SELECT 'city2' AS city, '1994-11-01' AS effective_date,
        SUM (authtaxrate) AS total_taxes
  FROM TaxRates AS R1
 WHERE R1.dteffective =
              (SELECT MAX (R2.dteffective)
                 FROM TaxRates AS R2
                WHERE R2.dteffective <= '1994-11-01'
                  AND R1.taxauthority = R2.taxauthority
                  AND R2.taxauthority
                        IN (SELECT taxauthority
                              FROM TaxAreaAuthority AS A1
                             WHERE A1.taxarea = 'city2'))
  GROUP BY city, effective_date;
```

Because the subquery is a noncorrelated, constant list, performance should be pretty good. And sure enough, when I look at the execution plan in WATCOM SQL, I find that the R1 and R2 tables were sequentially scanned, but the A1 table used the primary-key index. If I put indexes on the TaxRates table, I can get an even faster execution plan.

Diosdado Nebres, of Washington state, sent in an alternative solution to this puzzler:

```
SELECT SUM(T2.authtaxrate)
  FROM TaxAreaAuthority AS T1, TaxRates AS T2
 WHERE T1.taxarea = 'city2'
   AND T2.taxauthority = T1.taxauthority
   AND T2.dteffective =
           (SELECT MAX(dteffective)
              FROM TaxRates
             WHERE taxauthority = T2.taxauthority
               AND dteffective <= '1994-11-01');
```

He eliminated the GROUP BY, which is a good move, since the query will work as well—if not better—without it. And he replaced the deepest level of nesting with a JOIN between TaxAreaAuthority and TaxRates. That greatly reduces the number of times the first subquery is executed.

33 DEPRECIATION

This is based on a problem posted by Gerhard F. Jilovec on CompuServe. He had a manufacturing company database from which he wished to compute depreciation of the machinery. To this end, his database had a table of machines, like this:

```
CREATE TABLE Machines
(machine CHAR(20) NOT NULL PRIMARY KEY,
 purchasedate DATE NOT NULL,
 initialcost DECIMAL (10, 2) NOT NULL,
 lifespan INTEGER NOT NULL);
```

where the column purchasedate is just what you think—the purchase date of that machine. The initialcost column is for the initial cost of the machine. The lifespan column is for the expected lifespan of the equipment, given in days.

There is also a table of the cost of using a particular machine on a particular batch of work, defined as

```
CREATE TABLE ManufactCosts
(machine CHAR(20) NOT NULL REFERENCES Machines,
 manudate DATE NOT NULL,
 batch INTEGER NOT NULL,
 manucost DECIMAL (6,2) NOT NULL,
 PRIMARY KEY (machine, manudate, batch));
```

where the manudate column is the date that a particular batch was processed on that machine. The manucost is what it cost us for that batch. A similar table of manufacturing hours tells us how much time each batch took. It looks like this:

```
CREATE TABLE ManufactHrs
(machine CHAR(20) NOT NULL REFERENCES Machines,
 manudate DATE NOT NULL,
 batch INTEGER NOT NULL,
```

```
manuhrs DECIMAL(4,2) NOT NULL,
PRIMARY KEY (machine, manudate, batch));
```

Your problem is to suggest a better design for the database. Then you are to write a query that will give us the average hourly cost of each machine to date for any day we choose.

Answer

Time and money were in separate tables in the original design because the data was collected separately from time cards and from the accounting department.

You should put manufacturing cost (manucost) and manufacturing hours (manuhrs) in a single table, keyed by the machine, the date, and the batch number. If you can have hours without knowing the cost, or cost without knowing the hours, your design might allow NULLs in those columns, but you will still have to watch your math. I would replace the two tables with this:

```
CREATE TABLE ManufactHrsCosts
(machine CHAR(20) NOT NULL REFERENCES Machines(machine),
 manudate DATE NOT NULL,
 batch INTEGER NOT NULL,
 manuhrs DECIMAL(4,2) NOT NULL,
 manucost DECIMAL (6,2) NOT NULL,
 PRIMARY KEY (machine, manudate, batch));
```

Let's do an example with some data. We just bought a frammis cutter for $10,000 five days ago, and we were able to run seven batches on it. The lifetime for a frammis cutter is 1,000 days.

ManufactHrsCosts

machine	manudate	batch	manuhrs	manucost
'Frammis'	'1995-07-24'	101	2.5	123.00
'Frammis'	'1995-07-25'	102	2.5	125.00
'Frammis'	'1995-07-25'	103	2.0	110.00
'Frammis'	'1995-07-26'	104	2.5	125.00

(cont.)

machine	manudate	batch	manuhrs	manucost
'Frammis'	'1995-07-27'	105	2.5	120.00
'Frammis'	'1995-07-27'	106	2.5	120.00
'Frammis'	'1995-07-28'	107	2.5	125.00

On July 24, the first day of use, the average hourly cost was (($123.00 + $10.00)/2.5 hrs) = $127.00. But by July 25, the second day of use, the average hourly cost was ($123.00 + $125.00 + $110.00 +(2 * $10.00))/(2.5 + 2.5 + 2.0 hrs) = $55.43, a considerable reduction. At the end of the first five days, the hourly cost is $52.82 for the frammis cutter.

While you could do this with other approaches, I like to create a VIEW for total cost and hours. I can use it for other daily reports.

```
CREATE VIEW TotHrsCosts (machine, manudate, daycost, dayhrs)
 AS SELECT machine, manudate, SUM(manucost), SUM(manuhrs)
     FROM ManufactHrsCosts
     GROUP BY machine, manudate;
```

Let's assume we can compute the number of days between two DATE variables by subtraction. After that, your query is simply

```
SELECT :mydate, M1.machine,
 (((initialcost/lifespan)  -- amortized cost per day
  * (:mydate - M1.purchasedate + 1)) -- days of life so far)
 -- add the average hourly cost
 + (SELECT SUM(THC.daycost)/SUM(THC.dayhrs)
     FROM TotHrsCosts AS THC
     WHERE M1.machine = THC.machine)) AS hourly_cost
 FROM Machines AS M1
WHERE :mydate BETWEEN M1.purchasedate AND manudate;
```

Think about the WHERE clause predicate for a moment; it's a nice trick to avoid negative values in the first part of the calculations for hourly_cost.

34 CONSULTANT BILLING

Brian K. Buckley posted a version of the following problem on the PowerSoft CompuServe Forum in the WATCOM SQL section in November 1994, requesting assistance. He has three tables, defined as follows:

```
CREATE TABLE Consultants
(empid INTEGER NOT NULL,
 name CHAR(10) NOT NULL);
INSERT INTO Consultants
VALUES ((1, 'Larry'),
        (2, 'Moe'),
        (3, 'Curly'));

CREATE TABLE Billings
(empid INTEGER NOT NULL,
 effectdate DATE NOT NULL,
 billrate DECIMAL (5,2));

INSERT INTO Billings
VALUES ((1, '1990-01-01', 25.00);
        (2, '1989-01-01', 15.00),
        (3, '1989-01-01', 20.00),
        (1, '1991-01-01', 30.00));

CREATE TABLE HoursWorked
(jobid INTEGER NOT NULL,
 empid INTEGER NOT NULL,
 workdate DATE NOT NULL,
 billhours DECIMAL(5, 2));
```

```
INSERT INTO HoursWorked
VALUES ((4, 1, '1990-07-01', 3),
        (4, 1, '1990-08-01', 5),
        (4, 2, '1990-07-01', 2),
        (4, 1, '1991-07-01', 4));
```

He wanted a single query that would show a list of names and total charges for a given jobid. Total charges are calculated for each employee as the hours worked multiplied by the hourly billing rate applicable at the time the work was performed. For example, the sample data shown would give this answer:

Results

name	totalcharges
'Larry'	320.00
'Moe'	30.00

since Larry would have ((3+5) hours * $25 rate + 4 hours * $30 rate) = $320.00 and Moe (2 hours * $15 rate) = $30.00.

Answer #1

I think the best way to do this is to build a VIEW, then summarize from it. The VIEW will be handy for other reports. This gives you the VIEW:

```
CREATE VIEW HourRateRpt (empid, name, workdate, billhours,
                         billrate)
AS SELECT H1.empid, name, workdate, billhours,
        (SELECT billrate
           FROM Billings AS B0
          WHERE effectdate = (SELECT MAX(effectdate)
                                FROM Billings AS B1
                               WHERE B1.effectdate
                               <= H1.workdate
```

```
                                    AND B0.empid = B1.empid
                                    AND B0.empid = H1.empid))
    FROM HoursWorked AS H1, Consultants AS E1
    WHERE E1.empid = H1.empid;
```

Then your report is simply

```
SELECT empid, name, SUM(billhours * billrate) AS totbill
  FROM HourRateRpt
  GROUP BY empid, name;
```

But since Mr. Buckley wanted it all in one query, this would be his requested solution:

```
SELECT C1.empid, C1.name, SUM(billhours) *
(SELECT billrate
   FROM Billings AS B0
   WHERE effectdate = (SELECT MAX(effectdate)
                       FROM Billings AS B1
                       WHERE B1.effectdate <= H1.workdate
                       AND B0.empid = B1.empid
                       AND B0.empid = H1.empid))
  FROM HoursWorked AS H1, Consultants AS C1
  WHERE H1.empid = C1.empid
  GROUP BY C1.empid, C1.name;
```

This is not an obvious answer for a beginning SQL programmer, so let's talk about it. Start with the innermost query, which picks the effective date of each employee that immediately occurred before the date of this billing. The next level of nested query uses this date to find the billing rate that was in effect for the employee at that time; that is why the outer correlation name B0 is used. Then, the billing rate is returned to the expression in the SUM( ) function and multiplied by the number of hours worked. Finally, the outermost query groups each employee's billings and produces a total.

Answer #2

Linh Nguyen sent in another solution:

```
SELECT name, SUM(billhours*billrate)
    FROM Consultants AS C0, Billings AS B0, Hoursworked AS H0
    WHERE C0.empid = B0.empid
    AND C0.empid = H0.empid
    AND effectdate = (SELECT MAX(effectdate)
                          FROM Billings AS B1
                            WHERE B1.empid = C0.empid
                            AND B1.effectdate <= H0.workdate)
    AND H0.workdate >= effectdate
    GROUP BY name;
```

This version of the query has an advantage over the first solution in that it does not depend on SQL-92 features, such as subquery expressions, that many products do not yet have. The moral of the story is that you can get too fancy with new features.

PUZZLE

35 REQUISITION

This puzzle is a quickie in SQL-92, but very hard to do in SQL-89 and other database languages. Suppose you're in charge of the company inventory. You get requisitions that tell how many widgets people are putting into or taking out of a warehouse bin on a given date. Sometimes the quantity is positive (returns); sometimes it is negative (withdrawals).

```
CREATE TABLE Requisitions
(reqdate DATE NOT NULL,
 qty INTEGER NOT NULL CHECK (qty <> 0));
```

Your job is to provide a running balance on the quantity on hand as an SQL column. Your results should look like this:

Warehouse

reqdate	qty	qty_on_hand
'1994-07-01'	100	100
'1994-07-02'	120	220
'1994-07-03'	−150	70
'1994-07-04'	50	120
'1994-07-05'	−35	85

Answer #1

SQL-92 can use a subquery in the SELECT list, or even a correlated query. The rules are that the result must be a single value (hence the name "scalar subquery"), and if the query results are an empty table, the result is a NULL. This interesting feature of the SQL-92 standard sometimes lets you write an OUTER JOIN as a query within the SELECT clause. For example, the following query will work only if each customer has one or zero orders:

```
SELECT custno, custname,
            (SELECT orderamt
                FROM Orders
                WHERE Customers.custno = Orders.custno)
   FROM Customers;
```

and give the same result as

```
SELECT custno, custname, orderamt
  FROM Customers LEFT OUTER JOIN Orders
       ON Customers.custno = Orders.custno;
```

In this problem, you must sum all the requisitions posted up to and including the date in question. The query is a nested self-join, as follows:

```
SELECT reqdate, qty,
      (SELECT SUM(qty)
         FROM Requisitions AS R2
         WHERE R2.reqdate <= R1.reqdate) AS qty_on_hand
  FROM Requisitions AS R1
 ORDER BY reqdate;
```

Frankly, this solution will run more slowly than a procedural solution, which could build the current quantity on hand from the previous quantity on hand from a sorted file of records.

Answer #2:

Jim Armes, at Trident Data Systems, came up with a somewhat easier solution than the first answer:

```
SELECT R1.reqdate, R1.qty, SUM(R2.qty) AS qty_on_hand
  FROM Requisitions AS R2, Requisitions AS R1
 WHERE R2.reqdate <= R1.reqdate
 GROUP BY R1.reqdate, R1.qty
 ORDER BY R1.reqdate;
```

This query works, but becomes too costly. Assume you have (n) requisitions in the table. In most SQL implementations, the GROUP

BY clause will invoke a sort. Because the GROUP BY is executed for each requisition date, this query will sort one row for the group that belongs to the first day, then two rows for the second day's requisitions, and so forth until it is sorting (n) rows on the last day.

The "SELECT within a SELECT" approach in the first answer involves no sorting, because it has no GROUP BY clause. Assuming no index on the reqdate column, the subquery approach will do the same table scan for each date as the GROUP BY approach does, but it could keep a running total as it does. Thus, we can expect the "SELECT within a SELECT" to save us several passes through the table.

36 DOUBLE DUTY

Nigel Blumenthal posted a notice on CompuServe that he was having trouble with an application using PowerBuilder and WATCOM SQL. The goal was to take a source table of the roles that people play in the company, where 'D' means the person is a Director, 'O' means the person is an Officer, and we don't worry about the other codes. We want to produce a report with a code 'B' that means the person is both a Director and an Officer. The source data might look like this:

Roles

person	role
'Smith'	'O'
'Smith'	'D'
'Jones'	'O'
'White'	'D'
'Brown'	'X'

The result set will be:

Result

person	combined_role
'Smith'	'B'
'Jones'	'O'
'White'	'D'

Nigel's first attempt involved making a temporary table, but this was taking too long. Leonard C. Medal replied to this post with a query that could be used in a VIEW and save the trouble of building the temporary table. His attempt was something like this:

```
SELECT DISTINCT R1.person,
  CASE WHEN EXISTS (SELECT *
                    FROM Roles AS R2
```

```
                    WHERE R2.person = R1.person
                      AND R2.role IN ('D','O')) = 'D','O'
        THEN 'B'
        ELSE (SELECT R3.role
                FROM Roles AS R3
               WHERE R3.person = R1.person
                 AND R3.role IN ('D','O'))
     END AS combined_role
  FROM Roles AS R1
 WHERE R1.role IN ('D','O');
```

Can you come up with something better?

Answer #1

I was trying to mislead you into trying self-joins. Instead, you should avoid all those self-joins in favor of a UNION. The employees with a dual role will appear twice, so you're just looking for a row count of 2.

```
SELECT R1.person, MAX(R1.role)
  FROM Roles AS R1
 WHERE R1.role IN ('D','O')
 GROUP BY R1.person
HAVING COUNT(*) = 1
UNION
SELECT R2.person, 'B'
  FROM Roles AS R2
 WHERE R2.role IN ('D','O')
 GROUP BY R2.person
HAVING COUNT(*) = 2;
```

In SQL-92, you'll have no trouble putting a UNION into a VIEW, but some older SQL products may not allow it.

Answer #2

SQL-92 has a CASE expression and you can often use it as replacement. This leads us to the final, simplest form:

```
SELECT person,
       CASE WHEN COUNT(*) = 1
            THEN role
            ELSE 'B' END
  FROM Roles
 GROUP BY person;
```

The clause "THEN role" will work because we know that it is unique within a person, because it has a count of 1. However, some SQL products may want to see "THEN MAX(role)" instead, because "role" was not used in the GROUP BY clause, and they would see this as a syntax violation between the SELECT and the GROUP BY clauses.

PUZZLE
37 A MOVING AVERAGE

You are collecting statistical information stored by the quarter hour. What your customer wants is to get information by the hour—not on the hour. That is, we don't want to know what the load was at 00:00 Hrs, at 01:00 Hrs, at 02:00 Hrs, and so forth. We want the average load for the first four quarter hours (00:00, 00:15, 00:30, 01:00), for the next four quarter hours (00:15, 00:30, 01:00, 01:15), and so forth. This is called a moving average. We will assume that the sample table looks like this:

```
CREATE TABLE Samples
(sample_time TIMESTAMP NOT NULL PRIMARY KEY,
 load REAL NOT NULL);
```

Answer #1

One way is to add another column to hold the moving average:

```
CREATE TABLE Samples
(sample_time TIMESTAMP NOT NULL PRIMARY KEY,
 moving_avg REAL NOT NULL DEFAULT 0
 load REAL DEFAULT 0 NOT NULL);
```

Then update the table with a series of statements like this:

```
UPDATE Samples
   SET moving_avg
       = (SELECT AVG(S1.load)
            FROM Samples AS S1
           WHERE S1.sample_time
                 IN (Samples.sample_time,
                     (Samples.sample_time
                      - INTERVAL 15 MINUTES),
```

```
(Samples.sample_time
    - INTERVAL 30 MINUTES),
(Samples.sample_time
    - INTERVAL 45 MINUTES));
```

Answer #2

However, this is not the only way to write the UPDATE statement. The assumption that we are sampling exactly every 15 minutes is probably not true; there will be some sampling errors, so the timestamps could be a few minutes off. We could try for the hour time slot, instead of an exact match:

```
UPDATE Samples
   SET moving_avg
      = (SELECT AVG(S1.load)
           FROM Samples AS S1
          WHERE S1.sample_time
                BETWEEN (Samples.sample_time - INTERVAL 1 HOUR)
                    AND Samples.sample_time);
```

Answer #3

That last update attempt suggests that we could use the predicate to construct a query that would give us a moving average:

```
SELECT S1.sample_time, AVG(S2.load) AS avg_prev_hour_load
  FROM Samples AS S1, Samples AS S2
 WHERE S2.sample_time
       BETWEEN (S1.sample_time - INTERVAL 1 HOUR)
           AND S1.sample_time
 GROUP BY S1.sample_time;
```

Is the extra column or the query approach better? The query is technically better, because the UPDATE approach will denormalize the database. However, if the historical data being recorded is not going to change and computing the moving average is expensive, you might consider using the column approach.

CHAPTER

5

Grouping Data

SQL IS NOT a report-writer language. Yet it often has to act as a simple report writer that groups data into meaningful subsets. The reason for using SQL this way is that the server in a client/server system is usually much larger and much more powerful than the client machine. The more work that can be done on the server, the better the total performance.

The GROUP BY clause in SQL is not just a special kind of SELECT statement. The GROUP BY statement partitions the set into nonempty subsets that do not overlap. It then reduces each subset into one row made up of either the grouping values, scalar expressions, constants, or aggregate functions, or expressions built from these things. In short, a row in a grouped table contains information about the group, and not about any individual row in the table.

Most programmers start to solve a problem by sketching out the SELECT clause list, then writing all the tables that have the required values in the FROM clause, and finally thinking of a WHERE clause that will make it all happen. Loosely speaking, they are doing the equivalent in SQL pseudocode of asking, "What do I want? Where can I get it? How do I get it?"

However, there are situations where the best approach is to start with the GROUP BY clause to answer the question "What groups are we looking at?" and then move to the SELECT clause to ask "What do we want to know about these groups?"

PUZZLE

38 BUDGETING REPORT

Mark Frontera, of LanSoft, Inc., in Miami, Florida, posted a problem in the CompuServe WATCOM Forum in September 1995. He has budgeting information that consists of the following three tables: the items to be paid for, the estimated amounts to be spent on them, and the actual amounts spent on them. Notice that some items are covered by more than one check and sometimes one check covers several items.

Items

item_no	description
10	'item 10'
20	'item 20'
30	'item 30'
40	'item 40'
50	'item 50'

Actuals

item_no	actual_amount	check_no
10	300.00	'1111'
20	325.00	'2222'
20	100.00	'3333'
30	525.00	'1111'

Estimates

item_no	estimated_amount
10	300.00
10	50.00
20	325.00
20	110.00
40	25.00

I would like the following output from a single query:

Results

item_no	description	tot_act	tot_est	check_no
10	'item 10'	300.00	350.00	'1111'
20	'item 20'	425.00	435.00	'Mixed'
30	'item 30'	525.00	NULL	'1111'
40	'item 40'	NULL	25.00	NULL

Item 50 from the Items table is not to be shown, because there was no record for it in either the Actuals or the Estimates table. The column tot_act is the total of actual amounts for that item; the column tot_est is the total of estimated amounts for that item.

Answer

I think this schema needs some work, but you can do this with scalar subqueries and some tricky code.

```
SELECT I1.item_no, I1.description,
    (SELECT SUM (A1.actual_amount)

      FROM Actuals AS A1
     WHERE I1.item_no = A1.item_no) AS tot_act,
    (SELECT SUM (E1.estimated_amount)
      FROM Estimates AS E1
     WHERE I1.item_no = E1.item_no) AS tot_est,
    (SELECT CASE WHEN COUNT(*) = 1
               THEN MAX(check_no)
               ELSE 'Mixed' END
      FROM Actuals AS A2
     WHERE I1.item_no = A2.item_no
     GROUP BY item_no) AS check_no
 FROM Items AS I1
WHERE tot_act IS NOT NULL
   OR tot_est IS NOT NULL;
```

The trick is in the scalar subqueries. The first two calculate the total actual amounts and the total estimated amounts as if they were part of a GROUP BY and a LEFT OUTER JOIN.

The final subquery is trickier. The query finds all the Actuals that are associated with the item under consideration in the result table and makes a group from them. If the group is empty (no checks issued), the subquery returns a single NULL, and we display that NULL. If the group has one check in it, the CASE expression will return that single check number. The MAX( ) function is a safety check to guarantee that you have a scalar result from the subquery; you may not need it in all SQL-92 implementations. If more than one check is actually issued on the item, the COUNT(*) is greater than 1 and you get the string 'Mixed' instead of a string that represents the unique check number.

39 COUNTING FISH

Let's go fishing! A fish and game warden is trying to find the average of something that is not there. This is not quite as strange as it first sounds, nor quite as simple. The warden is collecting sample data on fish in the following table:

```
CREATE TABLE Samples
(sampleid INTEGER NOT NULL,
 fish CHAR(20) NOT NULL,
 numfound INTEGER NOT NULL,
 PRIMARY KEY (sampleid, fish));

INSERT INTO Samples
VALUES ((1, 'minnow', 18),
        (1, 'pike', 7),
        (2, 'pike', 4),
        (2, 'carp', 3),
        (3, 'carp', 9),
         ... );


CREATE TABLE SampleGroups
(groupid INTEGER NOT NULL,
 descript CHAR(20) NOT NULL,
 sampleid INTEGER NOT NULL,
 PRIMARY KEY (groupid, sampleid));

INSERT INTO SampleGroups
VALUES ((1, 'muddy water', 1),
        (1, 'muddy water', 2),
        (2, 'fresh water', 1),
        (2, 'fresh water', 3),
        (2, 'fresh water', 4),
         ...);
```

Notice that a sample can be grouped many ways; sample 1 is fresh muddy-water fish.

The warden needs to get the average number of each species of fish in the sample groups. For example, group number 1 ('muddy water') has samples 1 and 2; you could use the parameters (:myfish = 'minnow') and (:mygroup = 1) to find the average number of minnows in sample group 1, as follows:

```
SELECT fish, AVG(numfound)
  FROM Samples
 WHERE sampleid IN (SELECT sampleid
                      FROM SampleGroups
                     WHERE groupid = :mygroup)
   AND fish = :myfish
 GROUP BY fish;
```

This query will give you an average of 18 minnows, which is wrong. There were no minnows for sampleid 2 within group 1, so the average is ((18 + 0)/2) = 9. The other approach is to do several steps to get the correct answer: first use a SELECT statement to get the number of samples involved, then another SELECT to get the sum, and then manually calculate the average. Is there a way to do it in one SELECT statement?

Answer #1

The obvious answer is to enter a count of 0 for each fish under each sampleid, instead of letting it be missing. This approach will let you use the original query. You can create the missing rows with the following statement:

```
INSERT INTO Samples
SELECT M1.sampleid, M2.fish, 0
  FROM Samples AS M1, Samples AS M2
 WHERE NOT EXISTS (SELECT *
                     FROM Samples AS M3
                    WHERE M1.sampleid = M3.sampleid
                      AND M2.fish = M3.fish);
```

Answer #2

Unfortunately, it turns out that there are more than 100,000 different species of fish and tens of thousands of samples. This trick would fill up more disk space than the warden has. You need to use SQL-92 tricks to get it into one statement:

```
SELECT fish, SUM(numfound)/
          (SELECT COUNT(sampleid)
            FROM SampleGroups
           WHERE groupid = :mygroup)
  FROM Samples
 WHERE fish = :myfish
 GROUP BY fish;
```

The scalar subquery expression is really using the rule that an average is the total of the values divided by the number of occurrences. But the SQL is a little tricky.

The SUM( ) in the dividend returns a NULL when it has an empty set. This will make the fraction (quotient) become NULL. The scalar subquery expression in the divisor returns NULL when its result is an empty set. However, the COUNT(<expression>) aggregate function inside the subquery will return a zero when it has an empty set as its parameter.

The only way the COUNT(<expression>) aggregate function will return a NULL is from a table that has only NULLs in it. But we have declared all the tables to be without NULLs, so we're safe.

Answer #3

Anilbabu Jaiswal, of Kansas City, Kansas, submitted a slightly different Oracle version, which translates into SQL-92 as

```
SELECT fish, AVG(COALESCE(numfound, 0))
  FROM Samples AS SA
       LEFT OUTER JOIN
       SampleGroups AS SG
       ON SA.sampleid = SG.sampleid
```

```
     AND SA.fish = :myfish
     AND groupid = :mygroup
GROUP BY fish;
```

The COALESCE() function will inspect its parameter list and return the first non-NULL value, so this converts the AVG() parameter from NULL to zero. Most people seem to have trouble with the idea that an aggregate can handle an expression, not just a single column, as a parameter. The other good trick in this solution is doing a LEFT OUTER JOIN on two columns instead of just one. This is very handy, because the primary key of a table is not always just one column.

40 GRADUATION

Richard S. Romley created this problem based on the logic of a more complicated problem. It is a good example to show how we need to learn to analyze problems differently with ANSI/ISO SQL-92 stuff than we did before. There are some really neat solutions that didn't formerly exist if we learn to "think 92." This solution takes advantage of derived tables, CASE statements, and OUTER JOINs based on other than equality—all in one query.

In this problem, students take courses for which they receive credits. Each course belongs to a category. The Categories table lists each category and the minimum necessary credits in that category that are required for graduation. The CreditsEarned table has a row for each course completed, showing the student, category, and number of credits earned. (This would more logically contain student, course, and credits, and the category would be looked up in the Courses table, but for this problem I simplified the definition slightly.) The first problem is to generate a list of all students who are eligible to graduate—that is, those who have completed at least the minimum required credits in all categories. Then generate a list of all students who are not eligible to graduate. But best yet is to combine these two and generate a single list of all students, showing in the appropriate column whether or not each one is eligible to graduate.

EligibleReport

student	grad	nograd
Bob		X
Joe	X	
John		X
Mary	X	

```
CREATE TABLE Categories
(category CHAR(1) NOT NULL,
 rqd_credits INTEGER NOT NULL);
```

```
CREATE TABLE CreditsEarned
(student CHAR(10) NOT NULL,
 category CHAR(1) NOT NULL,
 credits INTEGER NOT NULL);

INSERT INTO Categories
VALUES (('A', 10),
       ('B', 3),
       ('C', 5));

INSERT INTO CreditsEarned VALUES ('Joe', 'A', 3);
INSERT INTO CreditsEarned VALUES ('Joe', 'A', 2);
INSERT INTO CreditsEarned VALUES ('Joe', 'A', 3);
INSERT INTO CreditsEarned VALUES ('Joe', 'A', 3);
INSERT INTO CreditsEarned VALUES ('Joe', 'B', 3);
INSERT INTO CreditsEarned VALUES ('Joe', 'C', 3);
INSERT INTO CreditsEarned VALUES ('Joe', 'C', 2);
INSERT INTO CreditsEarned VALUES ('Joe', 'C', 3);
INSERT INTO CreditsEarned VALUES ('Bob', 'A', 2);
INSERT INTO CreditsEarned VALUES ('Bob', 'C', 2);
INSERT INTO CreditsEarned VALUES ('Bob', 'A', 12);
INSERT INTO CreditsEarned VALUES ('Bob', 'C', 4);
INSERT INTO CreditsEarned VALUES ('John', 'A', 1);
INSERT INTO CreditsEarned VALUES ('John', 'B', 100);
INSERT INTO CreditsEarned VALUES ('Mary', 'A', 1);
INSERT INTO CreditsEarned VALUES ('Mary', 'A', 1);
INSERT INTO CreditsEarned VALUES ('Mary', 'A', 1);
INSERT INTO CreditsEarned VALUES ('Mary', 'A', 1);
INSERT INTO CreditsEarned VALUES ('Mary', 'A', 1);
INSERT INTO CreditsEarned VALUES ('Mary', 'A', 1);
INSERT INTO CreditsEarned VALUES ('Mary', 'A', 1);
INSERT INTO CreditsEarned VALUES ('Mary', 'A', 1);
INSERT INTO CreditsEarned VALUES ('Mary', 'A', 1);
INSERT INTO CreditsEarned VALUES ('Mary', 'A', 1);
```

```
INSERT INTO CreditsEarned VALUES ('Mary', 'A', 1);
INSERT INTO CreditsEarned VALUES ('Mary', 'B', 1);
INSERT INTO CreditsEarned VALUES ('Mary', 'B', 1);
INSERT INTO CreditsEarned VALUES ('Mary', 'B', 1);
INSERT INTO CreditsEarned VALUES ('Mary', 'B', 1);
INSERT INTO CreditsEarned VALUES ('Mary', 'B', 1);
INSERT INTO CreditsEarned VALUES ('Mary', 'B', 1);
INSERT INTO CreditsEarned VALUES ('Mary', 'B', 1);
INSERT INTO CreditsEarned VALUES ('Mary', 'C', 1);
INSERT INTO CreditsEarned VALUES ('Mary', 'C', 1);
INSERT INTO CreditsEarned VALUES ('Mary', 'C', 1);
INSERT INTO CreditsEarned VALUES ('Mary', 'C', 1);
INSERT INTO CreditsEarned VALUES ('Mary', 'C', 1);
INSERT INTO CreditsEarned VALUES ('Mary', 'C', 1);
INSERT INTO CreditsEarned VALUES ('Mary', 'C', 1);
INSERT INTO CreditsEarned VALUES ('Mary', 'C', 1);
```

This is the best solution I can come up with:

```
SELECT X.student,
       CASE WHEN COUNT(C.category)
                  >= (SELECT COUNT(*) FROM Categories)
            THEN 'X'
            ELSE ' ' END AS grad,
       CASE WHEN COUNT(C.category)
                  < (SELECT COUNT(*) FROM Categories)
            THEN 'X'
            ELSE ' ' END AS nograd
  FROM (SELECT student, category, SUM(credits) AS cat_credits
          FROM CreditsEarned
         GROUP BY student, category) AS X
       LEFT OUTER JOIN
       Categories AS C
       ON X.category = C.category
       AND X.cat_credits >= C.rqd_credits
 GROUP BY X.student;
```

Results

student	grad	nograd
Bob		X
Joe	X	
John		X
Mary	X	

The derived table X contains a row for each student, category, and total credits for that student/category combination. The key to this solution is in the next step—the LEFT OUTER JOIN to category on category and (credits >= required credits). By then grouping on student, COUNT(C.category) will tell me, for the categories in which the student took any courses, in how many he has at least the minimum number of credits required for graduation. By comparing this to the total number of categories, I can determine whether he is eligible to graduate and put the "X" in the appropriate column. This automatically handles the situation where a student may have taken no courses in a particular category. COUNT(C.category) will only count categories in which at least the minimum number of credits have been earned.

41 PAIRS OF STYLES

Abbott de Rham posted this problem on the MS-ACCESS Forum in September 1996. He gets data from sales slips that show pairs of styles in the order in which they are collected at the point of sale. The table looks like this:

```
CREATE TABLE SalesSlips
(style_a INTEGER NOT NULL,
 style_b INTEGER NOT NULL,
 tally INTEGER NOT NULL);
```

The table is arranged by the style that shows up first on an order as style_a; style_b is always the item that came after style_a on the order. The table will also include pairs in which the paired values are the same style.

Pairs

style_a	style_b	tally
12345	12345	12
12345	67890	9
67890	12345	5

For some of his reports, he would like to sum all pairs and their reciprocals together with a result set showing only one entry per pair:

Pairs

style_a	style_b	tally
12345	12345	12
12345	67890	14

He had no trouble getting records with reciprocals added together with a self-join, but he could not get rid of the duplicate records:

```
SELECT S0.style_a, S0.style_b, SUM(S0.tally + S1.tally)
    AS tally,
  FROM SalesSlips AS S0, SalesSlips AS S1
 WHERE S0.style_b = S1.style_a
   AND S0.style_a = S1.style_b
 GROUP BY S0.style_a, S0.style_b, S1.style_a, S1.style_b;
```

This returned false results:

Results

style_a	style_b	tally
12345	12345	24
12345	67890	14
67890	12345	14

He had considered writing code to seek the reciprocal, add the value, and delete a record while skipping style pairs with the same style numbers. He was hoping for an SQL solution instead.

Answer #1

The existing query can easily be patched up:

```
SELECT S0.style_a, S0.style_b, SUM(S0.tally + S1.tally) AS tally,
  FROM SalesSlips AS S0, SalesSlips AS S1
 WHERE S0.style_a <= S0.style_b
   AND S0.style_a = S1.style_b
   AND S0.style_b = S1.style_a
 GROUP BY S0.style_a, S0.style_b, S1.style_a, S1.style_b;
```

The self-join will be expensive and you really don't need it. In some SQL products (ACCESS is not one), you might be able to write

```
SELECT CASE WHEN style_a <= style_b
          THEN style_a
          ELSE style_b END AS s1,
```

```
        CASE WHEN style_a <= style_b
             THEN style_b
             ELSE style_a END AS s2,
        SUM (tally)
  FROM SalesSlips
 GROUP BY s1, s2;
```

Frankly, this is not supposed to work, because the column names s1 and s2 come into existence after the GROUP BY takes effect and therefore cannot be used by it. However, lots of products support this syntax because they improperly create the SELECT list first, then fill it. The correct SQL-92 version would use a tabular subquery:

```
SELECT s1, s2, SUM(tally)
  FROM (SELECT CASE WHEN style_a <= style_b
                    THEN style_a
                    ELSE style_b END,
               CASE WHEN style_a <= style_b
                    THEN style_b
                    ELSE style_a END,
               tally
          FROM SalesSlips) AS Report (s1, s2, tally)
  GROUP BY s1, s2;
```

Answer #2

In SQL-89, you would have to put the tabular subquery expression in a VIEW and then use the VIEW in another query. It's really the same code, but broken into separate steps and with the advantage that the VIEW can be reused for other reports.

```
CREATE VIEW Report (s1, s2, tally)
AS SELECT CASE WHEN style_a <= style_b
               THEN style_a
               ELSE style_b END,
```

```
              CASE WHEN style_a <= style_b
                   THEN style_b
                   ELSE style_a END,
             tally
       FROM SalesSlips;

SELECT s1, s2, SUM(tally)
  FROM Report
 GROUP BY s1, s2;
```

Answer #3

But the best way is to update the database itself and make `style_a` the smaller of the two code numbers before doing the query, so that this is not an issue:

```
UPDATE SalesSlips
   SET style_a = style_b,
       style_b = style_a
 WHERE style_a > style_b;
```

You could also do this with a TRIGGER on insertion.

PUZZLE

42 PEPPERONI

A good classic accounting problem is to print an aging report of old billings. Let's use the Friends of Pepperoni, who have a charge card at our pizza joint. It would be nice to find out whether you should have let club members charge pizza on their cards.

You have a table of charges that contains a member identification number (custid), a date (billdate), and an amount (amt). None of these is a key, so there can be multiple entries for a customer, with various dates and amounts. This is an old-fashioned journal file, done as an SQL table.

What you are trying to do is get a sum of amounts paid by each member within an age range. The ranges are 0 to 30 days old, 31 to 60 days old, 61 to 90 days old, and everything over 90 days old. This is called an aging report on accounts receivable, and you use it to see what the Friends of Pepperoni program is doing to you.

Answer #1

You can write a query for each age range with UNION operators, like this:

```
SELECT custid, '0-30 days = ' AS age, SUM (amt)
  FROM Friends Of Pepperoni
 WHERE billdate BETWEEN CURRENT_DATE
           AND (CURRENT_DATE - INTERVAL 30 DAY)
  GROUP BY custid
UNION
SELECT custid, '31-60 days = ' AS age, SUM (amt)
  FROM FriendsOfPepperoni
 WHERE billdate BETWEEN (CURRENT_DATE - INTERVAL 31 DAY)
           AND (CURRENT_DATE - INTERVAL 60 DAY)
  GROUP BY custid
UNION
SELECT custid, '61-90 days = ' AS age, SUM(amt)
  FROM FriendsOfPepperoni
```

```
  WHERE billdate BETWEEN (CURRENT_DATE - INTERVAL 61 DAY)
              AND (CURRENT_DATE - INTERVAL 90 DAY)
   GROUP BY custid
 UNION
 SELECT custid, '90+ days = ' AS age, SUM(amt)
   FROM FriendsOfPepperoni
  WHERE billdate < CURRENT_DATE - INTERVAL 90 DAY) GROUP BY custid
 ORDER BY custid, age;
```

Using the second column to keep the age ranges as text makes sorting within each customer easier, because the strings are in temporal order. This query works, but it takes a while. There must be a better way to do this in SQL-92.

Answer #2

Do not use UNIONs when you can use a CASE statement instead. The UNIONs will make multiple passes over the table; the CASE expression will make only one.

```
SELECT custid,
     SUM(CASE WHEN billdate
             BETWEEN CURRENT_TIMESTAMP - INTERVAL 30 DAYS
                 AND CURRENT_TIMESTAMP
             THEN amt ELSE 0.00) AS age1,
     SUM(CASE WHEN billdate
             BETWEEN CURRENT_TIMESTAMP - INTERVAL 60 DAYS
               AND CURRENT_TIMESTAMP - INTERVAL 31 DAYS
             THEN amt ELSE 0.00) AS age2,
     SUM(CASE WHEN billdate
             BETWEEN CURRENT_TIMESTAMP - INTERVAL 90 DAYS
                   AND CURRENT_TIMESTAMP - INTERVAL 61 DAYS
             THEN amt ELSE 0.00) AS age3,
     SUM(CASE WHEN billdate
                 < CURRENT_TIMESTAMP - INTERVAL 91 DAYS
             THEN amt ELSE 0.00) AS age4
  FROM FriendsofPepperoni;
```

Using the CASE expression to replace UNIONs is a handy trick.

43 PROMO

You have just gotten a job as the sales manager for a department store. Your database has the following two tables: one is a calendar of the promotional events the store has had, and the other is a list of the sales that have been made during the promotions. You need to write a query that will tell us which clerk had the highest amount of sales for each promotion, so that we can pay them a performance bonus.

```
CREATE TABLE Promotions
(promo CHAR (25) NOT NULL PRIMARY KEY,
 startdate DATE NOT NULL,
 enddate DATE NOT NULL);
```

Promotions

promo	startdate	enddate
'Feast of St. Fred'	'1995-02-01'	'1995-02-07'
'National Pickle Pageant'	'1995-11-01'	'1995-11-07'
'Christmas Week'	'1995-12-18'	'1995-12-25'

```
CREATE TABLE Sales
(clerk CHAR (15) NOT NULL,
 saledate DATE NOT NULL,
 amount DECIMAL (8,2) NOT NULL);
```

With this data:

Sales

clerk	saledate	amount
'Curly'	'1995-02-03'	250.99
'Curly'	'1995-02-03'	250.99
'Curly'	'1995-02-04'	100.00
'Curly'	'1995-02-05'	400.98
'Curly'	'1995-12-19'	400.98

	clerk	saledate	amount
(cont.)	'Curly'	'1995-12-20'	4.98
	'Larry'	'1995-02-03'	257.50
	'Larry'	'1995-02-04'	110.00
	'Larry'	'1995-02-05'	300.98
	'Larry'	'1995-11-01'	150.25
	'Larry'	'1995-11-01'	325.00
	'Larry'	'1995-11-02'	150.75
	'Larry'	'1995-12-23'	257.50
	'Larry'	'1995-12-24'	25.50
	'Moe'	'1995-11-01'	325.00
	'Moe'	'1995-11-01'	999.75
	'Moe'	'1995-11-03'	150.00
	'Moe'	'1995-12-18'	800.00
	'Moe'	'1995-12-19'	100.00
	'Moe'	'1995-12-20'	200.00
	'Moe'	'1995-01-04'	100.00

Answer #1

The trick in this query is that we need to find out what each employee sold during each promotion and finally pick the highest sum from those groups. The first part is a fairly easy JOIN and GROUP BY statement.

The final step of finding the largest total sales in each grouping requires a fairly tricky HAVING clause. Let's look at the answer first, then explain it.

```
SELECT S1.clerk, P1.promo, SUM(S1.amount) AS totsales
  FROM Sales AS S1 Promotions AS P1
 WHERE S1.saledate BETWEEN P1.startdate AND P1.enddate
 GROUP BY S1.clerk, P1.promo
```

```
HAVING SUM(amount) >=
    ALL (SELECT SUM(amount)
            FROM Sales AS S2
           WHERE S2.clerk <> S1.clerk
             AND S2.saledate
                 BETWEEN (SELECT startdate
                             FROM Promotions AS P2
                            WHERE P2.promo = P1.promo)
                     AND (SELECT enddate
                             FROM Promotions AS P3
                            WHERE P3.promo = P1.promo)
         GROUP BY S2.clerk);
```

We want the total sales for the chosen clerk and promotion to be equal to or greater than the other total sales of all the other clerks during that promotion. The predicate "S2.clerk <> S1.clerk" excludes the other clerks from the subquery total. The subquery expressions in the BETWEEN predicate ensure that we are using the right dates for the promotion.

The first thought, when trying to improve this query, is to replace the subquery expressions in the BETWEEN predicate with direct outer references, like this:

```
SELECT S1.clerk, P1.promo, SUM(S1.amount) AS totsales
  FROM Sales AS S1 Promotions AS P1
 WHERE S1.saledate BETWEEN P1.startdate AND P1.enddate
 GROUP BY S1.clerk, P1.promo
HAVING SUM(amount) >=
  ALL (SELECT SUM(amount)
          FROM Sales AS S2
         WHERE S2.clerk <> S1.clerk
           AND S2.saledate              -- Error !!
               BETWEEN P1.startdate AND P1.enddate
       GROUP BY S2.clerk);
```

But this will not work—and if you know why, you really know your SQL. Try to figure it out before you read further.

Answer #2

The "GROUP BY S1.clerk, P1.promo" clause has created a grouped table whose rows contain only aggregate functions and two grouping columns. The original working table built in the FROM clause ceased to exist and was replaced by this grouped working table, so the startdate and enddate also ceased to exist at that point.

However, the subquery expressions work, because they reference the outer table P1 while it is still available, since the query works from the innermost subqueries outward and not the grouped table. If we were looking for sales performance between two known, constant dates, the second query would work when we replaced P1.startdate and P1.enddate with those constants.

Two readers of my column sent in improved versions of this puzzle. Richard Romley and J. D. McDonald both noticed that the Promotions table has only key columns if we assume that no promotions overlap, so that using (promo, startdate, enddate) in the GROUP BY clause will not change the grouping. However, it will make the startdate and enddate available to the HAVING clause, thus:

```
SELECT S1.clerk, P1.promo, SUM(S1.amount) AS totsales
  FROM Sales AS S1 Promotions AS P1
 WHERE S1.saledate BETWEEN P1.startdate AND P1.enddate
 GROUP BY P1.promo, P1.startdate, P1.enddate, S1.clerk
HAVING SUM(S1.amount) >
    ALL (SELECT SUM(S2.amount)
          FROM Sales AS S2
         WHERE S2.Saledate BETWEEN P1.startdate AND P1.enddate
           AND S2.clerk <> S1.clerk
         GROUP BY S2.clerk);
```

Alternatively, you can reduce the number of predicates in the HAVING clause by making some simple changes in the subquery, thus:

```
    ...
HAVING SUM(S1.amount) >=
    ALL (SELECT SUM(S2.amount)
```

```
FROM Sales AS S2
WHERE S2.Saledate BETWEEN P1.startdate AND P1.enddate
GROUP BY S2.clerk);
```

I'm not sure whether there is much difference in performance between the two, but the second is cleaner. To give you a better feel for the data, here are the total sales per clerk for each promotion:

'Feast of St. Fred'

'Curly'	1002.96	<== Winner
'Larry'	668.48	
'Moe'	0.00	

'National Pickle Pageant'

'Curly'	0.00	
'Larry'	626.00	
'Moe'	1474.75	<== Winner

'Christmas Week'

'Curly'	405.96	
'Larry'	283.00	
'Moe'	1100.00	<== Winner

PUZZLE

44 BLOCKS OF SEATS

The original version of this puzzle came from Bob Stearns, at the University of Georgia, and dealt with allocating pages on an Internet server. I will reword it as a block of seat reservations in the front row of a theater. The reservations consist of the owner's name and the start and finish seat numbers of his block. The rule of ownership is that no two blocks can overlap. The table for the reservations looks like this:

```
CREATE TABLE Reservations
(owner CHAR(10) NOT NULL PRIMARY KEY,
 start INTEGER NOT NULL,
 finish INTEGER NOT NULL);
```

Reservations

owner	start	finish
'Eenie'	1	4
'Meanie'	6	7
'Mynie'	10	15
'Melvin'	16	18

What you want to do is put a constraint on the table to ensure that no reservations violating the overlap rule are ever inserted. This is harder than it looks unless you do things in steps.

Answer #1

The first solution might be to add a CHECK() clause. You will probably draw some pictures to see how many ways things can overlap, and you might come up with this:

```
CREATE TABLE Reservations
(owner CHAR(10) NOT NULL PRIMARY KEY,
 start INTEGER NOT NULL,
```

```
finish INTEGER NOT NULL,
CONSTRAINT No_Overlaps
 CHECK (NOT EXISTS
         (SELECT R1.owner
             FROM Reservations AS R1
           WHERE start BETWEEN R1.start AND R1.finish
             OR finish BETWEEN R1.start AND R1.finish)));
```

This is a neat trick that will also handle duplicate start and finish pairs with different owners, as well as overlaps.

Answer #2

There are two problems. Intermediate SQL-92 does not allow subqueries in a CHECK( ) clause, but full SQL-92 does allow them, so this trick probably won't work on your current SQL implementation. If you get around that problem, you may find that you have trouble inserting an initial row into the table. The PRIMARY KEY and NOT NULL constraints are no problem. However, when the engine does the CHECK( ) constraint, it will make a copy of the empty Reservations table in the subquery under the name R1.

Now things get confusing. The R1.start and R1.finish values cannot be NULLs, according to the CREATE TABLE statement, but D1 is empty, so they have to be NULLs in the BETWEEN predicates.

There is a very good chance that this self-referencing is going to confuse the constraint checker, and you will never be able to insert a first row into this table. The safest bet is to declare the table, insert a row or two, and add the No_Overlaps constraint afterward.

PUZZLE

45 UNGROUPING

Sissy Kubu sent me a strange question on CompuServe. She has a table like this:

```
CREATE TABLE Inventory
(goods CHAR(10) NOT NULL PRIMARY KEY,
 pieces INTEGER NOT NULL CHECK (pieces >= 0));
```

She wants to deconsolidate the table—that is, to get a VIEW or table with one row for each piece. For example, given a row with ('CD-ROM', 3) in the original table, she would like to get three rows with ('CD-ROM', 1) in each. Before you ask me, I have no idea why she wants to do this; consider it a training exercise.

Since SQL has no "UN-COUNT(*) ... DE-GROUP BY.." operators, you will have to use a cursor or the vendor's 4GL to do this. Frankly, I would do this in a report program instead of an SQL query, since the results will not be a table with a key.

The obvious procedural way to do this would be to write a routine in your SQL's 4GL that reads a row from the Inventory table, then writes the value of good to the second table in a loop driven by the values of pieces.

This will be pretty slow, since it will require (SELECT SUM(pieces) FROM Inventory) single-row insertions into the working table.

Can you do better?

Answer #1

I always stress the need to think in terms of sets in SQL. The way to build a better solution is to do repeated self-insertion operations, using a technique based on the "Russian peasant's algorithm," which was used for multiplication and division in early computers. You can look it up in a history of mathematics or a computer science book—it is based on binary arithmetic and can be implemented with right and left shift operators in assembly languages.

You're still going to need a 4GL to do this, but it won't be so bad. First, let's create two working tables and one for the final answer:

```
CREATE TABLE WorkingTable1
(goods CHAR(10) NOT NULL,
 pieces INTEGER NOT NULL);

CREATE TABLE WorkingTable2
(goods CHAR(10) NOT NULL,
 pieces INTEGER NOT NULL);

CREATE TABLE Answer
(goods CHAR(10) NOT NULL,
 pieces INTEGER NOT NULL);
```

Now start by loading the goods that have only one piece in inventory into the answer table:

```
INSERT INTO Answer
SELECT * FROM Inventory WHERE pieces = 1;
```

Now put the rest of the data into the first working table:

```
INSERT INTO WorkingTable1
SELECT * FROM Inventory WHERE pieces > 1;
```

This block of code will load the second working table with pairs of rows that each have half (or half plus one) of the piece counts of those in the first working table:

```
INSERT INTO WorkingTable2
SELECT goods, FLOOR(pieces/2.0)
 FROM WorkingTable1
WHERE pieces > 1
UNION ALL
SELECT goods, CEILING(pieces/2.0)
 FROM WorkingTable1
WHERE pieces > 1;
```

The FLOOR(x) and CEILING(x) functions return, respectively, the greatest integer that is lower than x and the smallest integer higher than x. If your SQL does not have them, you can write them with rounding and truncation functions. It's also important to divide by (2.0) and not by 2, because this will make the result into a decimal number.

Now harvest the rows that have gotten down to a piece count of one and clear out the first working table:

```
INSERT INTO Answer
 SELECT *
   FROM WorkingTable2
  WHERE pieces = 1;


DELETE FROM WorkingTable1;
```

Exchange the roles of WorkingTable1 and WorkingTable2, then repeat the process until both working tables are empty. That is simple, straightforward procedural coding. The way the results shift from table to table is interesting to follow. Think of these diagrams as an animated cartoon:

Step 1: Load the first working table, harvesting any goods that already had a piece count of one.

WorkingTable1		WorkingTable2	
goods	**pieces**	**goods**	**pieces**
'Alpha'	4		
'Beta'	5		
'Delta'	16		
'Gamma'	50		

The row ('Epsilon', 1) goes immediately to the Answer table.

Step 2: Halve the piece counts and double the rows in the second working table. Empty the first working table.

WorkingTable1

goods	pieces

WorkingTable2

goods	pieces
'Alpha'	2
'Alpha'	2
'Beta'	2
'Beta'	3
'Delta'	8
'Delta'	8
'Gamma'	25
'Gamma'	25

Step 3: Repeat the process until both working tables are empty.

WorkingTable1

goods	pieces
'Alpha'	1
'Alpha'	1
'Alpha'	1
'Alpha'	1
'Beta'	1
'Beta'	1
'Beta'	1
'Beta'	1
'Beta'	1
'Delta'	4
'Delta'	4
'Delta'	4
'Delta'	4
'Gamma'	12
'Gamma'	12
'Gamma'	13
'Gamma'	13

WorkingTable2

goods	pieces

'Alpha' and 'Beta' are ready to harvest

The cost of completely emptying a table is usually very low. Likewise, the cost of copying sets of rows (which are in physical blocks

of disk storage that can be moved as whole buffers) from one table
to another is much lower than that of inserting one row at a time.

The code could have been written to leave the results in one of
the working tables, but this approach allows the working tables to
get smaller and smaller, so that you get better buffer use. This
algorithm uses (SELECT SUM(pieces) FROM Inventory) rows of
storage and (log2((SELECT MAX(pieces) FROM Inventory)) + 1)
moves, which is pretty good on both counts.

Answer #2

Peter Lawrence, on CompuServe, suggested another answer to the
"uncount" problem. First create a table that contains all integers up
to at least the maximum number of pieces (n):

```
CREATE TABLE TallyTable (tally_nbr INTEGER NOT NULL);
INSERT INTO TallyTable VALUES ((1), (2), ..., (n));
```

Select the "uncount" as follows:

```
SELECT goods, 1 AS tally, tally_nbr
  FROM Inventory AS I1, TallyTable AS T1
 WHERE I1.pieces >= T1.tally_nbr
   AND T1.tally_nbr >= 1;
```

The results should be

Results

goods	tally	tally_nbr
'CD-ROM'	1	1
'CD-ROM'	1	2
'CD-ROM'	1	3
'Printer'	1	1
'Printer'	1	2

He finds a table like TallyTable above very useful and also
frequently has a temporal table containing, say, every hour of a
date/time range. This can be used for similar queries, such as selecting

every hour that someone was in the office when the database contains only the start and end times.

I like this answer, and the simple JOIN should be faster than my elaborate shuffle between two working tables. Mr. Lawrence was not the only reader of my *DBMS* column to find a solution using this method.

The only change I would make would be to play safe with the size of the TallyTable. First of all, we need to declare it with a primary key:

```
CREATE TEMPORARY TABLE TallyTable
(tally_nbr INTEGER NOT NULL PRIMARY KEY);
```

Mary Attenborough also came up with this solution, but her twist was a novel way of generating the table of consecutive numbers. This is another version of the Russian peasant's algorithm. Vinicius Mello then improved on this method of creating the working table further by simplifying the math involved. The procedure looks like this:

```
BEGIN
DECLARE maxnum INTEGER NOT NULL;
DECLARE ntimes INTEGER NOT NULL;
DECLARE increment INTEGER NOT NULL;

INSERT INTO TallyTable VALUES ((1), (2));

/* the count of rows in TallyTable doubles each loop */
SET maxnum = (SELECT MAX(pieces) FROM Inventory);
SET increment = 2;

WHILE increment < maxnum
    DO BEGIN
        INSERT INTO TallyTable
        SELECT tally_nbr + increment FROM TallyTable;
        SET increment = increment + increment;
        END;
END;
```

If we decide to make TallyTable permanent instead of loading it with a procedure, we'll need to see that some of the work gets done, leaving the items with a piece count greater than the highest tally_nbr still intact, thus:

```
SELECT goods, 1 AS tally, tally_nbr
  FROM Inventory AS I1, TallyTable AS T1
 WHERE I1.pieces >= T1.tally_nbr
   AND T1.tally_nbr BETWEEN 1 AND MAX(I1.pieces);
```

A second approach would be to reject the whole query if we have a piece count greater than the highest tally_nbr, thus:

```
SELECT goods, 1 AS tally, tally_nbr
  FROM Inventory AS I1, TallyTable AS T1
 WHERE I1.pieces >= T1.tally_nbr
   AND (SELECT MAX(I2.pieces) FROM Inventory AS I2)
       <= (SELECT MAX(T2.tally_nbr) FROM TallyTable AS T2);
```

The subquery expressions are known to be constant for the life of the query, so the optimizer can do them once by going to an index, in the case of the TallyTable, and with a table scan in the case of the Inventory table, since it is not likely to be indexed on the piece count.

Yet another way to generate the series of numbers is to remember how place-value notation works in Hindu-Arabic numbers. A list of numbers from 000 to 999 can be created by this code:

```
CREATE TABLE Digits (i INTEGER NOT NULL);
INSERT INTO Digits
VALUES ((0), (1), (2), (3), (4), (5), (6), (7), (8), (9));

INSERT INTO TallyTable
SELECT ((D1.i) + (10 * D10.i) + (100 * D100.i)) AS nbr
  FROM Digits AS D1, Digits AS D10, Digits AS D100
 WHERE nbr <= (SELECT MAX(pieces) FROM Inventory);
```

Obviously, you can extend this pattern to cover any size table you need. Warning! Do not simply throw more copies of the Digits table into the FROM clause to play safe. There is no optimizer smart enough to figure out when the query should stop, so it will generate all the numbers implied in the expression. Use a query to find the maximum number of pieces, and create only enough copies of Digits in the FROM clause to build numbers that will cover it.

PUZZLE

46 WIDGET

You get a production report from each work center that has a date, a center code, and the number of widgets produced from each batch of raw materials sent to the center that day. It looks like this:

```
CREATE TABLE Production
(center INTEGER NOT NULL,
 wkdate DATE NOT NULL,
 batchno INTEGER NOT NULL,
 widgets INTEGER NOT NULL,
 PRIMARY KEY (center, wkdate, batchno));
```

The boss comes in and wants to know the average number of widgets produced in all batches by date and center. You say "No problem" and do it. The next day, your boss comes back and wants the same data separated into three equal-sized batch groups. This sort of breakdown is important for certain types of statistical analysis of production work.

In other words, if on February 24, in center 42, you processed 21 batches, your report will show the average number of widgets made from the first seven batches, the second seven batches, and the last seven batches. Write a query that will show, by work center and date, the batch groups and the average number of widgets in each group.

Answer

The first query is straightforward:

```
SELECT center, wkdate, COUNT(batchno), AVG(widgets)
  FROM Production
 GROUP BY center, wkdate;
```

You have to make some assumptions about the second query. I am assuming batches are numbered from 1 to (n), starting over every day. If the number of batches is not divisible by 3, do a best fit that accounts for all batches. Using the CASE expression in SQL-92, you can find which third a batchno is contained in, using a VIEW, as follows:

```
CREATE VIEW Prod3 (center, wkdate, third, widgets)
   AS SELECT center, wkdate,
           CASE WHEN batchno <= MAX(batchno)/3 THEN 1
                WHEN batchno > (2*MAX(batchno))/3 THEN 3
                ELSE 2
           END, widgets
       FROM Production;
```

If you don't have this in your SQL, you might try something like this:

```
CREATE VIEW Prod3 (center, wkdate, third, batchno, widgets)
   AS SELECT center, wkdate, 1, batchno, widgets
       FROM Production AS P1
       WHERE batchno <= (SELECT MAX(batchno)
                          FROM Production AS P2
                          WHERE P1.center = P2.center
                          AND P1.wkdate = P2.wkdate)
   UNION
   SELECT center, wkdate, 2, batchno, widgets
     FROM Production AS P1
     WHERE batchno > (SELECT MAX(batchno)
                        FROM Production AS P2
                        WHERE P1.center = P2.center
                        AND P1.wkdate = P2.wkdate)
       AND batchno <= (SELECT 2 * MAX(batchno)
                        FROM Production AS P2
                        WHERE P1.center = P2.center
                        AND P1.wkdate = P2.wkdate)
   UNION
   SELECT center, wkdate, 3, batchno, widgets
     FROM Production AS P1
```

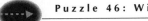

```
WHERE batchno > (SELECT 2 * MAX(batchno)
                   FROM Production AS P2
                  WHERE P1.center = P2.center
                    AND P1.wkdate = P2.wkdate);
```

Either way, you end up with this final query:

```
SELECT center, wkdate, third, COUNT(batchno), AVG(widgets)
  FROM Prod3
 GROUP BY center, wkdate, third;
```

PUZZLE

47 TWO OUT OF THREE

We are putting together an anthology with contributions from many contributors (identified by their contrnum). As it works out, we want to find all contributors who have articles in exactly two out of three categories in the book for a specified set of three categories that we put into the query as parameters.

```
CREATE TABLE Anthology
(contrnum INTEGER NOT NULL PRIMARY KEY,
 contributor CHAR(20) NOT NULL,
 category INTEGER NOT NULL,
 ... );
```

Answer #1

The first thought is that this is a simple GROUP BY query that would look like this:

```
SELECT contrnum, contributor, :1st_cat, :2nd_cat, :3rd_cat
  FROM Anthology AS A1,
 WHERE A1.category IN (:1st_cat, :2nd_cat, :3rd_cat)
 GROUP BY contrnum, contributor
HAVING COUNT(*) = 2;
```

But this will not work, because one contributor might have made two contributions in only one area. What you needed was a COUNT(DISTINCT <expression>) aggregate function. This is still a very easy query:

```
SELECT contrnum, contributor, :1st_cat, :2nd_cat, :3rd_cat
  FROM Anthology AS A1,
 WHERE A1.category IN (:1st_cat, :2nd_cat, :3rd_cat)
 GROUP BY contrnum, contributor
HAVING COUNT(DISTINCT A1.category) = 2;
```

Can you find other ways of doing this without using a GROUP BY? I'm not recommending any of the following solutions; the point of this exercise is to make you appreciate the GROUP BY clause.

Answer #2

The specification does not tell whether we want *any* two of the three categories, or a particular order (for example, category 1 and category 2, but not category 3). The latter is actually easy to do:

```
SELECT A1.contrnum, A1.category, A2.category
  FROM Anthology AS A1,
       Anthology AS A2
 WHERE A1.contrnum = A2.contrnum    -- self-join table
   AND A1.category = :1st_category  -- category #1 first
   AND A2.category = :2nd_category  -- category #2 second
   AND NOT EXISTS (SELECT *         -- but no category #3
                                    -- anywhere
                    FROM Anthology AS A3
                   WHERE A1.contrnum = A3.contrnum
                     AND A3.category = :3rd_category));
```

Answer #3

But the query to find any two out of three has to rely on some tricky coding. This answer will not tell you which two of the three is missing, however:

```
SELECT contrnum, contributor, :1st_cat, :2nd_cat, :3rd_cat
  FROM Anthology AS A1,
 WHERE A1.category IN (:1st_cat, :2nd_cat, :3rd_cat)
   AND EXISTS
       (SELECT *
          FROM Anthology AS A2,
         WHERE A2.category IN (:1st_cat, :2nd_cat, :3rd_cat)
```

```
        AND A1.category < A2.category
        AND A1.contrnum = A2.contrnum
        AND NOT EXISTS
              (SELECT *
                FROM Anthology AS A3,
               WHERE A3.category
                     IN (:1st_cat, :2nd_cat, :3rd_cat)
                   AND A1.contrnum = A3.contrnum
                   AND (A1.category <> A3.category
                        OR A2.category <> A3.category)));
```

To find the contributors who have something in all three categories, just change the NOT EXISTS( ) to EXISTS( ).

To find the contributors who have only one category:

```
SELECT contrnum, contributor, :1st_cat
  FROM Anthology AS A1,
 WHERE A1.category = :1st_cat
   AND NOT EXISTS (SELECT *
                    FROM Anthology AS A2
                   WHERE A2.category = :1st_cat
                     AND A1.contrnum = A2.contrnum
                     AND A1.category <> A2.category);
```

which is a "collapsed version" of the two-out-of-three query.

PUZZLE

48 BUDGET VERSUS ACTUAL

C. Conrad Cady posted a simple SQL problem on the CompuServe Gupta Forum. He has two tables, Budgeted and Actual, which describe how a project is being done. Budgeted has a one-to-many relationship with Actual. The tables are defined like this:

```
CREATE TABLE Budgeted
(task INTEGER NOT NULL PRIMARY KEY,
 category INTEGER NOT NULL,
 est_cost DECIMAL(8,2) NOT NULL);

CREATE TABLE Actual
(voucher DECIMAL(8,2) NOT NULL PRIMARY KEY,
 task INTEGER NOT NULL REFERENCES Budgeted(task),
 act_cost DECIMAL(8,2) NOT NULL);
```

He wants a Budgeted-versus-Actual comparison for each category. This is easier to see with an example:

Budgeted

task	category	est_cost
1	9100	100.00
2	9100	15.00
3	9100	6.00
4	9200	8.00
5	9200	11.00

Actual

voucher	task	act_cost
1	1	10.00
2	1	20.00
3	1	15.00

(cont.)

voucher	task	act_cost
4	2	32.00
5	4	8.00
6	5	3.00
7	5	4.00

The output he wants is this:

Result

category	estimated	spent
9100	121.00	77.00
9200	19.00	15.00

The $121.00 is the sum of the est_cost of the three task items in category 9100. The $77.00 is the sum of the act_cost of the four voucher items related to those three task items (three amounts are related to the first item, one to the second, and none to the third).

He tried this query:

```
SELECT category, SUM(est_cost) AS estimated,
               SUM(act_cost) AS spent
 FROM (Budgeted LEFT OUTER JOIN Actual
      ON Budgeted.task = Actual.task)
 GROUP BY category;
```

and he got

Result

category	estimated	spent
9100	321.00	77.00
9200	31.00	15.00

The problem is that the $100.00 is counted three times in the JOIN, giving $321.00 instead of $121.00, and the $11.00 is counted twice, giving $31.00 instead of $19.00 in the JOIN.

Is there a simple, single piece of SQL that will give him the output he wants, given the above tables?

Answer

Bob Badour suggested that he can get the required result by creating a VIEW in SQL-89:

```
CREATE VIEW cat_costs (category, est_cost, act_cost)
AS SELECT category, est_cost, 0.00
     FROM Budgeted
   UNION
   SELECT category, 0.00, act_cost
     FROM Budgeted, Actual
    WHERE Budgeted.task = Actual.task;
```

followed by this query:

```
SELECT category, SUM(est_cost), SUM(act_cost)
  FROM cat_costs
 GROUP BY category;
```

In SQL-92, we can JOIN the total amounts spent on each task to the category in the Budgeted table, like this:

```
SELECT B1.category, SUM(est_cost), SUM(spent)
  FROM Budgeted AS B1
       LEFT OUTER JOIN
       (SELECT task, SUM(act_cost) AS spent
          FROM Actual AS A1
        GROUP BY task)
       ON A1.task = B1.task
 GROUP BY B1.category;
```

The LEFT OUTER JOIN will handle situations where no money has been spent yet. If you have a transitional SQL that does not allow subqueries in a JOIN, extract the subquery shown here and put it in a VIEW.

49 PERSONNEL PROBLEM

Daren Race was trying to aggregate the results from an aggregate result set using Gupta's SQLBase and could not think of any way other than using a temporary table or a VIEW. This is an example of what he was doing:

Personnel

name	deptid
Daren	Acct
Joe	Acct
Lisa	DP
Helen	DP
Fonda	DP

Then he viewed the data as an aggregate by deptid:

```
SELECT deptid, COUNT(*)
 FROM Personnel
 GROUP BY deptid;
```

The results will be

Result

deptid	COUNT(*)
Acct	2
DP	3

Then he wanted to find the average department size! The way he did this was to use a VIEW:

```
CREATE VIEW DeptView (deptid, tally)
AS SELECT deptid, COUNT(*)
  FROM Personnel
  GROUP BY deptid;
```

Then

```
SELECT AVG(tally) FROM DeptView;
```

He asked if anyone on the Gupta Forum on CompuServe could think of a way of doing this without using temporary tables (or VIEWs). He got two answers, namely

```
SELECT AVG(DISTINCT deptid)
 FROM Personnel;
```

and

```
SELECT COUNT(*) / COUNT(DISTINCT deptid)
 FROM Personnel;
```

Your problem is to tell me what is wrong with each of them.

Answer

The first answer will grab the department numbers, throw away NULLs (there should not be any in this case), then throw away duplicates and average what is left. This has nothing to do with the number of people in each department; we will get (1+2/2) = 1.5 for an answer.

The second answer is really much better and will give us the right results for this data. We have a COUNT(*) = 5, and COUNT(DISTINCT deptid) = 2, so the answer we get is (2.5), just as we wished.

But now we hire three new employees, Larry, Moe, and Curly, who are not yet assigned to a department, and our table looks like this:

Personnel

name	deptid
Daren	Acct
Joe	Acct
Lisa	DP
Helen	DP
Fonda	DP
Larry	NULL
Moe	NULL
Curly	NULL

We now have a COUNT(*) = 8, but COUNT(DISTINCT deptid) = 2 because it drops NULLs, so the answer we get is (4). The real answer is that we cannot determine an exact value, but we know that it is between (8/5 = 1.60) and (8/3 = 2.66), depending on what we do with Larry, Moe, and Curly.

If Mr. Race had stuck to his original method, we would have gotten

Result

deptid	COUNT(*)
Acct	2
DP	3
NULL	3

and a final result of 1.5 as before, because the NULLs would form a group by themselves in the VIEW, but then would be dropped out by the average in the final query.

50 PLAYING THE PONIES

You have just become the database manager for Mafia boss Eddie Franco ("the Doctor") Coddetti. He keeps records on horse races for statistical purposes and his basic table looks like this:

```
CREATE TABLE RacingResults
(track CHAR(3) NOT NULL,
 racedate DATE NOT NULL,
 race INTEGER NOT NULL,
 win CHAR(30) NOT NULL,
 place CHAR(30) NOT NULL,
 show CHAR(30) NOT NULL,
 PRIMARY KEY (track, date, race));
```

The track column shows the name of the track where the race was held, racedate is when it was held, race is the number of the race, and the other three columns are the names of the horses that won, placed, and showed for that race.

The Doc comes to you one day and he wants to know how many times each horse was in the money. What SQL query do you write for this?

Answer #1

The phrase "in the money" means that the horse won, placed, or showed in a race—we don't care which. The first step is to build a VIEW with the aggregate information, thus:

```
CREATE VIEW InMoney (horse, tally, position) AS
SELECT win, COUNT(*), 'win'
  FROM RacingResults
 GROUP BY win
UNION
SELECT place, COUNT(*), 'place'
  FROM RacingResults
```

```
GROUP BY place
UNION
SELECT show, COUNT(*), 'show'
  FROM RacingResults
GROUP BY show;
```

Now use that view to get the final summary:

```
SELECT horse, SUM(tally)
  FROM InMoney
GROUP BY horse;
```

The reason for putting those string constants on the side is so that if Doc Coddetti wants to know how many times each horse finished in each position, you can just change the query to

```
SELECT horse, position, SUM(tally)
  FROM InMoney
GROUP BY horse, position;
```

Answer #2

If you have a table with all the horses in it, you can write the query as

```
SELECT H1.horse, COUNT(*)
  FROM HorseNames AS H1, RacingResults AS R1
 WHERE H1.horse IN (R1.win, P1.place, R1.show)
GROUP BY H1.horse;
```

The nice part is that you will also see the horses that never got in the money.

PUZZLE

51

HOTEL ROOMS

Ron Hiner put this question on the WATCOM Forum on CompuServe. He had a data conversion project where he needed to automatically assign some values to be used as part of the PRIMARY KEY to a table of hotel rooms.

The floor part of the PRIMARY KEY is the FOREIGN KEY to another table of floors within the building. The part of the hotel room key we need to create is the room number, which has to be a sequential number, starting at $x01$ for each floor x. The hotel is small enough that we know we will have only three-digit numbers. The table is defined as follows:

```
CREATE TABLE Hotel
(floor SMALLINT NOT NULL,
 room SMALLINT NOT NULL,
 PRIMARY KEY (floor, room),
 FOREIGN KEY floor REFERENCES Bldg(floor);
```

Currently, the data in the table looks like this:

floor	room
1	NULL
1	NULL
1	NULL
2	NULL
2	NULL
3	NULL

WATCOM (like some other versions of SQL) has a NUMBER(*) function that begins at 1 and returns an incremented value for each row that calls it.

Is there an easy way, via the NUMBER(*) function (or some other means), to automatically populate the room column? Mr. Hiner was thinking of somehow using a GROUP BY floor-number clause to restart the numbering back at 1.

Answer #1

The WATCOM support people came up with this approach. First make one updating pass through the whole database, to fill in the room numbers. This trick will not work unless you can guarantee that the Hotel table is updated in sorted order. As it happens, WATCOM can guarantee just that with a clause on the UPDATE statement, thus:

```
UPDATE Hotel
   SET room = (floor*100)+NUMBER(*)
 ORDER BY floor;
```

which would give these results:

floor	room
1	101
1	102
1	103
2	204
2	205
3	306

followed by

```
UPDATE Hotel
   SET room = (room - 3)
 WHERE floor = 2;
```

```
UPDATE Hotel
   SET room = (room - 5)
 WHERE floor = 3;
```

which would give the correct results:

floor	room
1	101
1	102
1	103

floor	room
2	201
2	202
3	301

(cont.)

Unfortunately, you have to know quite a bit about the number of rooms in the hotel. Can you do better without having to use the ORDER BY clause?

Answer #2

I would use SQL to write SQL statements. This is a neat trick that is not used enough. Just watch your quotation marks when you do it and remember to convert numerics to characters, thus:

```
SELECT DISTINCT
       'UPDATE Hotel SET room = ('
       || CAST (floor AS CHAR(1))
       || '* 100)+NUMBER(*) WHERE floor = '
       || CAST (floor AS CHAR(1)) || ';'
 FROM DummyTable;
```

This statement will write a result table with one column that has a test, like this:

```
UPDATE Hotel SET room = (floor*100)+NUMBER(*) WHERE floor = 1;
UPDATE Hotel SET room = (floor*100)+NUMBER(*) WHERE floor = 2;
UPDATE Hotel SET room = (floor*100)+NUMBER(*) WHERE floor = 3;
    . . .
```

Copy this column as text to your interactive SQL tool, or into a batch file, and execute it. This does not depend on the order of the rows in the table.

You could also put this into the body of a stored procedure and pass the floor as a parameter. You are going to do this only once, so writing and compiling a procedure is not going to save you anything.

About the Author

Joe Celko is an Atlanta-based consultant with Northern Lights Software Ltd., has been a member of the ANSI X3H2 Database Standards Committee since 1987, and helped write the ANSI/ISO SQL-89 and SQL-92 standards.

Mr. Celko has published several regular monthly or biweekly columns in the past 11 years in the computer trade and academic press. His current columns are "SQL Explorer" in *DBMS* (Miller Freeman), "WATCOM SQL Corner" in *Powerbuilder Developers' Journal* (SysCon), and "Celko on Software" in *Computing* (VNC Publications, UK).

Most recently, Mr. Celko has written "Celko on SQL" in *Database Programming & Design* (Miller Freeman), "SQL Puzzle" in *Boxes and Arrows* (Frank Sweet Publishing), "DBMS/Report" in *Systems Integration* (Cahner-Ziff), "Data Desk" in *Tech Specialist* (R&D), and "Data Points" in *PC Techniques* (Coriolis Group), and has been the editor of the "Puzzles & Problems" section of *Abacus* (Springer-Verlag).

He is the author of two books on SQL, both of which came out in 1995: *SQL for Smarties* (Morgan Kaufmann) and *Instant SQL* (Wrox Press). His next book in the Morgan Kaufmann series will be on data and database fundamentals and principles.

Mr. Celko is a regular speaker and an SQL instructor for Digital Consulting Inc., Norm DiNardi Enterprises, Boston University Corporate Education Center, and Miller Freeman Seminars.

INDEX